Meet Me

WRITERS IN ST. LOUIS

Meet Me

WRITERS IN ST. LOUIS

INTERVIEWS BY
CATHERINE RANKOVIC

PenUltimate Press, Inc.
Saint Louis, Missouri

Publisher: PenUltimate Press, Inc.
Design/Production: Renée Duenow
Printer: BookMasters, Inc.

On the Cover: Home of Alan and Mary Ann Zaggy, St. Louis, Missouri
Cover Photography: Renée Duenow

PenUltimate Press, Inc.
520 North Skinker Boulevard
Saint Louis, Missouri 63130
Phone: (314) 862-3842
Fax: (314) 862-0045
E-mail: penultim@swbell.net
Web: www.penpressinc.org
Book Site: www.meetmewritersinstlouis.com

Library of Congress Control Number: 2009907533

Rankovic, Catherine, 1957
Meet Me: Writers in St. Louis
pp. 152
ISBN   0-9760675-4-4
ISBN 13   978-0-9760675-4-2
1. Literature 2. Writers

Printed in the United States

10 9 8 7 6 5 4 3 2 1

To live by a large river is to be kept in the heart of things.
JOHN HAINES

Contents

Introduction

Every man is a moon and has a side which he turns toward nobody;
you have to slip around behind if you want to see it.

MARK TWAIN

Crossing paths with as many great writers as I have is a miracle. Meeting some of them, and having been able to ask them questions and preserve their answers, is purely and simply a grant. With this book I can share my good fortune with you.

I was trained as a journalist so I could make gainful my interest in writing and literature. The saying "Journalism is literature in a hurry" implies that literature is the parent art and journalism its restless child. But journalism is also a child of Clio, muse of history. I did these interviews for hire but collected them because I feel responsible to history. Without *Meet Me* the interviews originally published before the digital era—before about 1997—would exist only in microforms, if that, and in scattered archives. They would be as good as lost. I couldn't let that happen.

That is because I am convinced that the literary activity clustered around St. Louis at the turn of this century has produced writers and work so very fine, so diverse and remarkable, that I think St. Louis rivals the Paris of the storied 1920s, and I made this book looking forward to the day when everyone will agree with me. Ambiance aside, St. Louis may even surpass in richness the old moveable feast: The St. Louis party has lasted much longer, and many writers from elsewhere have chosen to settle in the area. About Paris in the '20s we have many primary sources, but readers, historians, and biographers curious about that era's most iconic writers might have keenly appreciated a collection of interviews, preferably all by one reliable person with no ax to grind. I hope *Meet Me* shows that I took my role seriously. Langston Hughes's fictional everyman, named Simple, once said, "I listened fluently." I did something like that.

I came to St. Louis in 1988 to study poetry in the Master of Fine Arts in Writing (M.F.A.) program at Washington University. I stayed because St. Louis offered low rents, congenial employment, chances to write what I wanted, and a warmhearted literary community anchored and fed by the area's several universities, most of them now with graduate programs in creative writing. Washington University in St. Louis stands out in this collection because it is where I met and worked with many of the writers in *Meet Me*.

St. Louis has a distinguished literary heritage. Edgar Allan Poe wanted to come to St. Louis to edit a literary magazine. Mark Twain wished he had bought the place. Feminist heroine Kate Chopin, and Eugene Field, the children's poet, lived here. Theodore Dreiser was a journalist here. T. S. Eliot's grandfather founded Washington University—and born here too were Marianne Moore, Martha Gellhorn, William Burroughs, A. E. Hotchner, and Maya Angelou. Tennessee Williams was laughed out of college here; I used to walk past the site of his old apartment building every day. New Yorkers Howard Nemerov and Stanley Elkin lived and worked in St. Louis and thought it pretty darned fine; I heard them say so. I am friends with at least thirty St. Louis writers whose books, popular or literary, should be better known. If I could pick one trait that marks St. Louis writers, it would be honesty. Almost everyone in *Meet Me* speaks of it.

Communicators by profession, tuned to their inner promptings, writers are a pleasure to interview. I am grateful to have been granted some of their time, because writers prefer writing to discussing the writing process or their inner lives. It is true that not everyone in town got interviewed. Writing for news outlets requires an occasion for an interview, such as a writer's new book or change of status, events that would be deemed newsworthy. The more recent interviews fill what I consider inexcusable gaps in the record—gaps unfilled by anyone else. I might have done more, asked harder questions, but I trust in the value of what is here: writers speaking in the first person singular.

As a young journalist I was urged to believe that there was something noble about—and this is what journalism feels like—digging around near the foundations of the world and letting it be known what I had found. In St. Louis I saw writers inspiriting an American city that threatened at the turn of this century to sunder itself or rust out. I met writers who fought for the independence of literature. I learned that what is made well and strictly today will likely be around tomorrow.

CATHERINE RANKOVIC
APRIL, 2009
ST. LOUIS, MISSOURI

Meet Me
WRITERS IN ST. LOUIS

Eric
Pankey

POET

From *Apocrypha*

IN MEMORY

If the world is created from the Word,
What can I hear amid the noise of that one
Assertion and all that rattles and diminishes

In its wake: the mockingbird's trill and grate,
The sluice and overlap where the creek narrows,
The dragonfly needling through the humid air?

And what will I hear when words are no more?
I cannot hear you now, ash-that-you-are,
My beloved, who in your passion and error,

In what was your life gave life to me,
My life from the life of your blunt body
That is no more. If I believe that Christ

Is risen, why can't I believe that we too
Will be risen, rejoined, and relieved
Of the world's tug and the body's ballast?

We are asked to testify, to bear
Witness to what we have seen and heard,
And yet our hope is in the veiled and silenced.

I take comfort in your silence,
In the absence of the voice that voiced your pain.
The body apart from the spirit is dead

But that does not mean the spirit is dead.

Apocrypha, New York: Knopf, 1991. Used with permission.

This interview captures Eric Pankey, age 32, just crystallizing his identity as a "devotional poet." *Apocrypha*, the book of poems published at the time of this interview, was the first of three Pankey books employing Christian imagery and written in dense and referential language that invited comparison with the poetry of Wallace Stevens—except that they lacked the playful element. Like Christianity itself, even when celebratory, Pankey's poems were sober and demanding; they put serious mileage on the reader. From the interview it is clear that I must have complained to him about that.

Pankey met me at the St. Louis Amtrak station one evening in May 1988, becoming the first St. Louisan as well as the first St. Louis writer I met. The following day I met his Washington University colleague Howard Nemerov, jubilant over having just been named U. S. Poet Laureate.

Pankey is a graduate of the University of Iowa's writing program. In addition to the three books mentioned in this interview, Pankey published *The Late Romances* (1997) and *Cenotaph* (2000) with Knopf. *Oracle Figures* (2003), *Reliquaries* (2005), and *The Pear as One Example: New and Selected Poems* (2008) were published by Ausable Press.

Pankey has received several significant fellowships, including those from the National Endowment for the Arts and the Guggenheim Foundation. In 1996 he left Washington University to become a professor of English at George Mason University in Fairfax, Virginia.

"To Eat, Drink, and Sleep Poetry and Not Feel Like an Oddball"

First published in *The Riverfront Times*, Nov. 20, 1991

Tall, thin, wheat-colored, bespectacled, seated at a desk in the pointedly functional office he shares with poet Donald Finkel, poet Eric Pankey is at his day job. "This is about as good as it gets. Decent city, decent salary," he says. Too, there are the famous colleagues, and three months off every summer to write. Pankey directs Washington University's creative writing program. His job makes him a living. His poetry is making him a notable name.

Pankey's third book, *Apocrypha*, a gorgeous Knopf hardback, is just out. The publisher matters: Knopf's poetry list is exclusive and highbrow. His first book, *For the New Year* (1984), written while a student at the University of Iowa Writers' Workshop, won a national competition. He freed himself from high school teaching with a grant, producing *Heartwood* (1988). For years now, poems by this native of Raytown, Mo., have appeared in the most rarified of literary quarterlies, and he has a coveted contract with *The New Yorker*. Pankey is just 32, and so qualifies as a boy wonder.

It hasn't gone to his head. He's shy, quiet to inaudibility, as self-conscious as a teenager; thus, perhaps, the obscurantist beard and glasses. He blushes. He weighs his words. There are now very few poets of his kind; you get the sense he wishes there were more. At some level he must be ambitious and determined, but only his list of publications would prove it in a court of law. Maybe once a year, as he will on Dec. 9, at Duff's, he'll do a local reading.

"It's not like I can sell a poem and pay the mortgage," Pankey says, about making a living. "The best I can do is sell a poem and maybe buy a dryer—I did that last year. My primary job is administrative, though I spend time as a teacher here. I think it's very exciting that so much good poetry, and some great poetry, is being written in a marketplace that isn't warm to it."

About the only warm welcome poets can expect these days is at universities with creative writing programs. Because of an oversupply of candidates, jobs like Pankey's are hard to snag. Pankey has directed the writing program for four years, hosting guest professors, budgeting, phoning, meeting, counseling graduate students ("Of course they don't have time to write. Who does?"), and reading through an avalanche of applications. Increasingly, he teaches. Summers, he and his wife, poet Jennifer Atkinson, retreat to Connecticut for four hours a day of intensive writing for each. That's as good as it gets. They have a young daughter. During the school year, he can at most revise poems and send them out—poetry's necessary drudge work.

"I really feel that if I'm anywhere it's because of doggedness," says Pankey, who, prodded by a high school teacher, published his first poem at age 15. "Once a poem is finished, or seems finished, it's out looking for a home continually."

Pankey's story is not quite one of systematic, businesslike progress toward his goals. Eric's parents were accountants. He was their youngest child.

"When I was a little kid, I wanted to be a cartoonist, doing, like, a panel in the newspaper," Pankey says. "So I drew a lot, and of course with cartoons you have to also write. Reading comic books led to reading other books, and somewhere along the line I started checking out books of poetry.

"The first poem I remember writing was in the sixth grade. A teacher, Mrs. Redeker, accused me of having copied it out of a book. That made me assume the poem must be good, if she thought someone else had written it. And then of course I suffered the usual elementary school injustice: Because I was a plagiarist, I didn't get to go out to the playground. So," Pankey says, smiling a little, "I've dedicated my life to reclaiming that 15-minute recess."

Pankey's parents, unperturbed by their son's impractical bent, encouraged him. So did teachers. Pankey prepared for a career teaching English.

"I've followed the traditional pattern, insofar as the last 30 years is traditional of young American poets," Pankey says. "I didn't study creative writing as an undergraduate, but I went to a graduate school. What I found there was just a lot of people like I was, interested in poetry, and it was wonderful to have two years to eat, drink, and sleep poetry and not feel like an oddball."

The manuscript of *For the New Year*, which Pankey now calls "apprentice work," won a Walt Whitman Award from the Academy of American Poets shortly after Pankey's graduation from Iowa. The prestigious prize included publication. This is the kind of break most young writers pant for. "It seems to me that writers don't necessarily deserve a break. They may earn a break, but they don't deserve one just because they write," Pankey says, making it clear he believes himself an earner.

Yet it's unusual to publish poems, much less a book of poems, at age 25; Pankey's success is, first, exceptional. Persistence keeps it that way. Work in the academy—where some critics think poets ought not to be—permits continued accomplishments.

"I don't know if it's the best place," Pankey says. "It's a good place, because at least the people in the academy care about literature. A good portion of them built their careers paying attention to poetry, whether or not they give the living poets the same reverence. The nice thing about the university is that they think writing is part of your job. You won't find corporations necessarily offering that kind of benefit.

"I don't think I write because I have to. I don't at all. But I write because it's interesting and exciting to me. I wish that angels would talk to me, put poems in my head, but they don't. It's really hard work, but it's interesting. It's very much like solving a problem. Language is absolutely inadequate to give shape to everything we think and feel."

The new book's title, *Apocrypha*, is defined as "writings, usually religious, of doubtful origin or authenticity." As the choice of title suggests, it isn't an easy read. *Heartwood* simply and transparently recalled a Missouri boyhood; *Apocrypha* charts spiritual territory, on the border of the obscure.

"I don't know if every poem in the book adds up to this," Pankey explains, "but the general concern is the possibility of faith in the world, trying to distinguish between the qualities of doubt and the qualities of faith. They're poems confronting questions of spirituality without in any way wanting to be inspirational or devotional or evangelical. They're about what we can know and can't know." To a charge that the poems are difficult, he responds, "Poems aren't immoral because of their difficulty.

"The poems since *Apocrypha* are finding themselves to be a little more direct in the way they're presenting information. And I'm trying to confront some content I've dealt with before, and that's thinking about the life of the body."

Harper
Barnes

NOVELIST

From *Blue Monday*

SETTING: KANSAS CITY, APRIL, 1935. LATE AT NIGHT.

Teddy's long legs were angled up against the dashboard and he began slapping a steady, driving beat against his right thigh—*pop, pop, pop, pop*. Libba picked up the beat and began to hum—that's not the right word, think of the sound a bumblebee makes and give it the resonance of human bone. . .

We could see the lights and hear the music and shouting on 12th Street a couple of blocks before we got there and, at the intersection, it hit like an explosion. We turned right and for three short blocks—Vine, Highland, Woodland—12th Street was swarming with life, like a carnival midway on Saturday night.

Music blasted from half a dozen clubs or storefronts along the stretch of low brick and frame buildings, and hundreds of people were on the street, drinking, eating, bouncing along, leaning in doorways of clubs to hear the music for free, shouting at each other—"Hey, baby, how you been?"—hugging each other and slapping flesh, dancing in the street. It was like the last few buoyant hours of Mardi Gras in a village that was deadly serious about Lent, or a round-up time celebration in a wide-open frontier town, except this happened almost every night along 12th and 18th streets.

With his drumming right hand, Teddy switched from his thigh to the dashboard and drove harder into the beat. With his left he reached across Libba to flick little accents on the horn every time some heedless celebrant would wander in front of the car.

Blue Monday, Tooele, UT: Patrice Press, 1991. Used with permission.

F amiliar to St. Louisans as a music and movie critic for the daily *St. Louis Post-Dispatch*, and often called that paper's best writer, Harper Barnes had for 20 years wanted to write and publish a novel, and did so in 1991. Titled *Blue Monday*, it remains Barnes' only novel. Nonetheless that places him among the few professional journalists who have actually published the novels they always say they will write.

Associated with the *Post-Dispatch* since 1965, a full-timer since 1974, Barnes in 1997 took early retirement and became the editor of *St. Louis Magazine*, a monthly that in earlier incarnations had failed to find its audience. This move surprised his readers who did not know that in the early 1970s Barnes had been called on to edit and likewise save New England's flagship alternative weekly, *The Boston Phoenix*. Barnes stabilized *St. Louis Magazine*, seeking out and publishing essays by St. Louis writers of national stature such as humorist David Carkeet and historian Wayne Fields. Barnes left *St. Louis Magazine* on January 1, 2000, to work as a freelance critic and feature writer. In 2001 he published a highly regarded historical biography titled *Standing on a Volcano: The Life and Times of David Rowland Francis* (Missouri Historical Society Press), using research amassed by the great-grandson of this colorful St. Louis politician, civic booster, and organizer of the 1904 St. Louis World's Fair, who gave his name to Francis Field and Francis Park. Barnes' history of the 1917 East St. Louis race riots, *Never Been a Time,* was published in 2008.

In this interview, Barnes says, "We're all in the movies," but only long after this interview did it become generally known that as a handsome youth Barnes acted the starring role in an educational film about venereal disease, *Innocent Party* (Centron, 1959) uttering the memorable line: "I've got a sort of sore—down there!" This mini-drama, filmed in Lawrence, Kansas, was shown to millions of students in "hygiene" or "sex ed" classes during the 1960s and is now the subject of serious study and a cult classic.

"First Novel, by a Middle-Aged Guy"

First published in *The Riverfront Times,* Oct. 30, 1991

Harper Barnes, the Post-Dispatch's jazz-loving critic-at-large, turns novelist this week with the publication of *Blue Monday* (Patrice Press). Set in Kansas City in 1935, the novel follows a hard-drinking, club-crawling cub reporter, Michael Holt, and his investigation into the death of real-life jazz bandleader Bennie Moten, whose actual death on April 2, 1935, at age 38, has never been adequately explained.

CATHERINE RANKOVIC: *Let's start out with the beginnings of your career in journalism.*

HARPER BARNES: I came to St. Louis in 1965. I'd been a teaching assistant at the University of Kansas, where my major was English. I had no journalistic background. The *Post-Dispatch* said, well, why don't you write a story? We'll give you a chance. There had been a civil rights demonstration sit-in at the University of Kansas in 1964, and they hired me on the basis of that story. I think I was helped by the fact that Bill Woo [William Woo, in 1991 the *Post-Dispatch's* editor-in-chief] at the time was a feature writer at the "Everyday Magazine." Bill and I had been roommates at the University of Kansas; I think Bill put in a good word for me.

So I worked for the *Post-Dispatch* from '65 to '70. I started out on general assignment, and in '68 I became the pop-music critic. Then in 1970 a friend of mine from Kansas City bought a struggling six-month-old underground newspaper in Boston called the *Phoenix* and asked me to come work for him. So I spent two years editing the *Phoenix*. I got fired in 1972. The problem was that the man who owned the paper wanted to have more control, and he finally decided the only way to get it was to fire me. In essence, it was a question of control of the paper. Virtually the entire staff, including the comptroller, walked out. They ended up getting their union recognized, but I had to step down. The owner ended up signing a deal with the union that gave it a great deal of control over both hiring and editorial policy.

At the end of it I stayed in Boston for another year and a half and was a free-lance writer. Late in '73 I came back here; there was a newspaper starting here, and I edited this interim paper, put out by the staffs of the *Post* and *Globe*. It was called *St. Louis Today*. In '74 I came back to work for the *Post-Dispatch*, and I've been there ever since.

You've been working on the novel since the early '80s.

Yeah. I took a leave in 1981 and '82 and worked on it for 10 months, wrote a very rough first draft. Then I came back to work. I worked on it for another couple of years and sent it off to New York, say around '83. All of these very encouraging letters told me, in effect, "The writing is great, the plot's screwed up." I think they were right. Anyway, I put it away for a while and fooled around with a mystery novel, which was a total disaster. But I learned what not to do. And also—I don't know if you want to know this—I had a real drinking problem. About five or six years ago, after I got divorced, and that's a long, complicated story, I met Roseann (Weiss, Barnes' wife, an art dealer), and I quit drinking. She encouraged me to rewrite the novel, so I did.

At that point it was late '89 or early '90, and the New York publishing business—none of the people who'd read the book was around, or those that were weren't at all interested anymore in reading a first novel, by a middle-aged guy, about Kansas City. I couldn't even get anybody to read it. I sent queries to six or eight places. Only two publishers actually saw the entire manuscript. One was a very commercial publisher who said it wasn't commercial enough, and the other was a very literary publisher who said it wasn't literary enough.

I decided this was silly, and I'd noticed that Patrice Press, which is local, had done a good job on some other books, and I knew that Greg Franzwa, who owns Patrice, was a jazz fan—in fact, an amateur jazz musician. So I sent it to Greg last winter. I guess maybe I just didn't want to keep getting all this rejection from New York. Oh, maybe if I'd pursued it—now I realize that people get 50 rejection slips and keep going, but (*laughs*) two was enough for me. And as it turned out, Greg was the perfect person to publish the book. I had a very serious mistake in there about jazz improvisation that Greg corrected. And Greg was here, so I had input on the cover, input on marketing.

Obviously, it'd be nice to have Random House or whatever, because you get the national distribution. But on the other hand, I've talked to people who've had big publishers, and they talk about how they get just completely lost in the shuffle. Anyway, I'm real happy with the way it's gone.

I'm interested in the inspiration behind this novel. Is it anything more than a love for jazz? You have a lot of mystery-story and detective-story elements in it.

I'm a fan of mystery novels. A lot of prose in there is reminiscent of Chandler and Hammett, I think. And one of the things the very literary house objected to was that Chandler-Hammett prose. They even suggested that I rewrite it without that. I feel the prose is central to the theme of the book, because one of the things this book is about is that this boy and girl (fictional *Kansas City Journal-Post* reporter Michael Holt, and his girlfriend, Rachael Loeb) have both read too many mystery stories. He kind of thinks he's Philip Marlowe, she kind of thinks she's Miss Marple or something, and that's one of their problems. I mean, life isn't a mystery story.

I didn't know why I wrote it that way the first time I wrote it. And I went back and I thought, well, this is why: This is exactly the way this guy would tell this story. He would tell it in that tone, because that's the way he's looking at it, as if he were a detective in a hard-boiled novel. As it turns out, he gets totally screwed up, because life isn't a hard-boiled novel.

I think part of the book is about life imitating fiction. I talk about the gangsters, about how you couldn't tell whether the gangsters were imitating Scarface or Scarface was imitating the gangsters. One of the most fascinating things about America in the 20th century—and it's almost impossible to deal with novelistically, without seeming like you're writing about other fiction or movies—is the fact that we interact with movies particularly, fiction in general. We're all influenced by popular culture. I think even the love scenes we play with people we really love are influenced by it.

This very literary publisher kept saying, "These characters are like characters in the movies!" And I kept trying to explain—well, you can't explain. Either you get it or you don't. My point was, of course, that's what the second two-thirds of the 20th century in America has been all about. We're all in the movies.

You talked about a failed novel that you did after the first draft of Blue Monday. *Had you done any creative writing before that?*

After I got fired, my first wife and I lived on the seacoast north of Boston, and I gazed out the window at the sea crashing over the rocks and tried to write a novel, an autobiographical novel, and it just didn't work. It was mush. It wasn't tied to anything. I was trying to be James Joyce, trying to write *Portrait of the Artist as a Young Man.* I didn't realize you had to connect it to actual events. It was all off the top of my head. So I decided, when I started *Blue Monday* six or seven years later, to tie it down very specifically to historical events, because otherwise I have a tendency just to float away and write all of this lyrical stuff that people think, "Oh, isn't that beautiful," but how much of that can you read? This is really the first novel I ever got more than 50 pages into.

You must have studied English back in Kansas for a reason. Was that because you wanted to be a novelist?

I've always wanted to be a novelist. I've always thought of myself as a novelist. And it's been scary. It's scary because you're out there. As a novelist, you're very much exposing yourself, and the first negative review I'll probably have problems with. There's something arrogant about wanting someone to read 210 pages of something I made up.

I guess secretly I've always thought of myself as a novelist who happened to be working at a newspaper. I've tried to be good (*laughs*) at the newspaper stuff, but this is something else.

So you got the time to do the first draft of the novel by taking a 10-month leave. And then, in the years between, how did you get time to write?

I did it in the mornings. There's a lot of historical research that went into the book, and I had to really totally immerse myself in the period to write the first draft. Once I did that, I had something down, and then you can work an hour or two every morning because you've got a framework.

But it did take a very long time.

I think I got delayed by the other novel; I know I lost a couple years because I was drunk. And I rewrote a lot. And the characters kept doing things on me. It was my first novel, so I didn't know how to control the characters. They'd start doing this weird stuff! One person said, you set up in the first chapter this idea there's going to be a romance between Michael and Libba, the black pianist who's based on Mary Lou Williams. I started writing the scene in which he made a pass at her. I didn't know what was going to happen. I think what she did rings true, but it was like automatic writing.

You're working on a novel about Pretty Boy Floyd.

The reason I'm interested in Pretty Boy Floyd is I think he personified the outlaw-hero to the poor people of the Depression. If the book is influenced by anything, it'd be Woody Guthrie's song "Pretty Boy Floyd" and Steinbeck's *The Grapes of Wrath*, because Floyd was the hero of the Okies, and I think mythical outlaws are very important. I think the yuppies of the '80s and '90s find outlaws offensive. I think it's crucial to America to believe in outlaws. If we're going to have an individualistic society, then we've got to be brave individuals. I don't mean we have to go out and stick up banks, but I mean our heroes ought to be people of courage and daring, people who are not afraid to break the law. I mean, certainly in the '60s and '70s I broke the law a lot, both for political reasons and because I smoked marijuana. And I tend to relate to outlaws.

But not the kind of outlaws we have in St. Louis that three blocks from my house murdered a man and his pregnant wife last night.

Obviously, that's the intellectual—that's the problem with the metaphor. At least Floyd, in his early days, was a kind of Robin Hood. He later turned into a much more vicious killer. And I want to deal with why somebody who started out as a pretty decent guy, who became a crook because he was poor, turned into this hired killer. The guy who killed the pregnant woman in your neighborhood, that's not the kind of outlaw I'm talking about.

When can we look for this novel?

I don't know. Maybe a couple years. And I may not do it. I'm having real problems with it, partly for the reasons you suggest. In the newspaper, there's a report that Floyd began his criminal career in St. Louis in 1925 by holding up a Kroger payroll for $12,000. I found he was accused, along with three or four companions—it's a little unclear, but it seems to be statutory rape, involving some women camping on the Meramec River. I don't want my hero to be a rapist. Not at that point, at least. I could see that happening later, because I think that many, many people get corrupted, but—so I'm having problems. I'm not trying to make him politically correct; I'm having trouble dealing with that concept of a hero.

Tess Gallagher

POET

From *Amplitudes*

WOMEN'S TUG OF WAR AT LOUGH ARROW

In a borrowed field they dig in their feet
and clasp the rope. Balanced
against neighboring women, they hold
the ground by the little gained
and leaning like boatmen rowing into
the damp earth, they pull
to themselves the invisible waves, waters
overcalmed by desertion
or the narrow look trained to a brow.

The steady rain has made girls of them,
their hair in ringlets. Now they haul
the live weight to the cries
of husbands and children, until the rope
runs slack, runs free
and all are bound again by the arms
of those who held them, not until, but so
they gave.

Amplitudes, St. Paul: Graywolf Press, 1987. Used with permission.

For this interview, done while Tess Gallagher was in St. Louis to promote two new books, I was able to describe what was on her and Raymond Carver's coffee table because I had been to their house and seen it. At Syracuse University, Gallagher taught a graduate course called "Poetry in Translation," and I was one of her students. In the spring of 1988 Tess and her companion Raymond Carver hosted a party celebrating her new book, *Amplitudes: Poems Selected and New,* culled from her first three books of poetry. That was the first and last time I met Carver. The star instructor of the university's master's-level creative writing program for some years, he was off doing something else when I got to Syracuse. His fiction, labeled "minimalism," made me think: Steinbeck divided by Hemingway = Ray Carver. I preferred Tess's poetry. She wrote lovely, liquid lines. She'd also published essays and short fiction. Unlike any other female writer I had met, she knew her own worth and never devalued herself. She was even glamorous. Citing the example of Anna Akhmatova, she told our class, "Part of being a great poet is having great pictures taken of yourself." But behind her glamour was substance. It was like the glamour of royalty.

Carver was then fatally ill, and meek, and murmurous; a small man further diminished by suffering. Nonetheless he was scheduled to do a public reading of his work in the near future and was taking suggestions as to what to read. Carver's story collection *Cathedral* (1983) and the selected stories collection *Where I'm Calling From* (1988), had pulled all the right levers for all the right people, catapulting him, and Tess, on a world tour, and into the pages of gossipy *People* magazine. Then Carver developed lung cancer, and died August 2, 1988, at age 50.

When I met Gallagher in St. Louis for this interview, four years had passed, and I wondered beforehand if she would remember me. Of course she did.

Gallagher was born in Washington State and attended the University of Washington, receiving a B.A. degree in education in 1967, and an M.A. in English in 1971. Since the time of this interview she has published *At the Owl Woman Saloon: Stories* (Scribners, 1999), another volume of selected poems, *My Black Horse* (Bloodaxe Books, 2000), and a volume of selected stories. *Moon Crossing Bridge* was reissued by Graywolf in 2002. Fourteen years elapsed between the time of this interview and Gallagher's next book of new poems, *Dear Ghosts* (Graywolf, 2006).

"The Nuclear Physics of Loss"

First published in *The Riverfront Times*, June 3, 1992

"We really did have a life that was bound up in each other's work," says poet Tess Gallagher of her nine-year association with fiction writer Raymond Carver, who died of lung cancer in 1988. Together they became a literary industry, with Carver writing the best fiction of his life and dabbling in poetry, and Gallagher writing her prizewinning poetry and a book of short stories, recently reissued, titled *The Lover of Horses* (Graywolf Press); both wrote essays and officially collaborated on a screenplay.

Their partnership brought them media attention of the kind serious writers rarely get. They were written up in *Vanity Fair* and *People* and proudly displayed these magazines on the coffee table in their home in Syracuse, N.Y. Carver had taught fiction writing at Syracuse University, Jay McInerney (*Bright Lights, Big City*) being his best-known disciple, and Gallagher taught poetry writing there from 1980 through 1989. Through translations of their work and invitations to South America, Europe, and Japan, they were becoming international literary figures. In this first, belated rush of fame, Carver fell ill.

The two married in a Las Vegas wedding chapel shortly before Carver's death; it was his second marriage and her third. Gallagher, now 49, has since worked to complete and publish Carver's unfinished projects, and it is, unfortunately, for this that she is most widely (I almost wrote "wifely") known. It is ironic, and sexist, she said, that work wholly her own should be assessed in the light of her relationship with Carver. Gallagher, author of four previous books of poetry, has just published two utterly astonishing new books, *Moon Crossing Bridge* (Graywolf) and *Portable Kisses* (Capra), the first a powerful exploration of widowhood and love beyond death, and the second a series of playful love poems that test the limits of the lyric. They are nothing like her previous work, accomplished as it was. If *Moon Crossing Bridge* has an analogue in American poetry, it would have to be Sylvia Plath's *Ariel*, such is its originality and daring.

Gallagher, who was born and now lives in Port Angeles, Washington, recently made her first visit to St. Louis, the last of 12 cities on a national tour. Her mother, Georgia Morris Bond, is a southwest Missouri native, so Gallagher felt, she said, at home. Gallagher is a dramatic presence, with her colleen's bright-white skin, waist-length black hair, penciled brows and sweet, symbolic jewelry: a crystal heart pendant, red enamel heart-shaped earrings, a silver ring that is the subject of a poem in *Moon Crossing Bridge*, and—still—her gold wedding band. Roland Barthes' *A Lover's Discourse* lay bookmarked on the motel-room bed. Asked to autograph *Portable Kisses* ("Ideally," she wrote in its introduction, "a reader should finish this book, then find somebody to kiss"), she inscribed it with her favorite fountain pen, then lipsticked her mouth and signed the title page with a dark pink kiss mark.

CATHERINE RANKOVIC: *Will you tell us how* Moon Crossing Bridge *got written?*

TESS GALLAGHER: I began to write it in January of 1989. I had just done a lot of work on Ray's last book, *A New Path to the Waterfall*, in the sense of really getting it to press. I was asked to write an introduction, and that hadn't been part of what Ray and I thought to do with the book. But because his death came so early—he was only 50—and because he was ending with a book of poems instead of stories, and because the book was a kind of joint making in the sense that I worked with him very closely on the drafts, I thought it would be honest and good to place the poems in the kind of time in which they occurred and in that relationship.

I wrote a few of the *Moon Crossing Bridge* poems in January of '89, just enough so I sensed there was a large body of material. It was the first time I had done this in my writing. I felt if I didn't attend to it, I would lose it. I thought I needed at least three years to do what I had to do, so I attempted to get a leave of absence. But in universities there's no such thing as a three-year leave, so Syracuse just politely told me that wasn't possible, and I then decided to resign. I didn't resign without thought, because I loved my vocation as a teacher also. But I really wanted to write these poems. I was writing and working on the book right up into September 1991.

There was a point at which I thought the book was pretty well finished, and that was with the poem "Glow." That was overturned by the fact that I continued to write poems all through spring and summer of last year. The result of that was this little book, *Portable Kisses*, and the sixth section of *Moon Crossing Bridge*, which I originally thought might be going into *Portable Kisses*. I talked to my editor about this and decided to move them into *Moon Crossing Bridge*. I think it was the right thing to do. It sort of got us across the bridge entirely in those last poems. Both books went to press simultaneously.

The books give the impression of having been written by two different people.
Portable Kisses has a wryness of spirit and loquaciousness and angularity, perhaps. And sensuality. And wit, not in the light sense, but in the sense of somebody who sees all sides of something. And that side of me that just likes to delight, that loves the pure lyric.

There's much more risk-taking with language in these two new books than in your previous books. How do you account for that?

I guess when you've faced the mortality of the person you loved most in the world, and fought the kind of battle we did in those 10 months, you've thrown everything you've had into an ultimate situation. You think, "Why not? Why not do this at its highest pitch? Why not require the most?" After all, the most is required of us in this life. So I didn't worry about even writing something that wouldn't be readable, in the sense that it would be costly to people's psychic energies and how much they could volunteer of their emotions. It's not a hobbyist's book.

You've written a great deal about Ray, have appeared in two documentaries about Ray's life, and have written the text for the book Carver Country. *Don't you find this takes energy away from your own work?*

Yes, it does. But I've found ways to handle it. I hired a secretary, for one thing. I realized I was doing the work of two, the living for two. Those were very necessary things to do, I think, and I was the only one who could do them. Ray had begun the *Carver Country* book, and so it was up to me to finish it.

What's your response to the criticism you've received for finishing so much of Ray's work and spending so much time living in his reputation?

It looks different to me than it does to others, because I of course remember the beginning of the relationship. I remember having had quite a career as a poet behind me, and being better known as a poet than Ray was, actually, as a fiction writer at the time we met. There was a coterie of fiction aficionados who knew about Ray, but Ray did not really get well known until after *Cathedral* came out in 1983.

When I first started to live with him in El Paso in 1979, and I wanted to go to Alaska, I told them there, "There's this man I'm attached to, and I want him to be able to come there if I come. Can you possibly find a venue for him? He's a fiction writer, Raymond Carver," and they said, "Raymond who?" He had his first job down there in Texas, in El Paso, after he got sober. Nobody was offering him much at all; El Paso is not the center of the literary world. In 1981 I was to go to Zurich for a week or two, and when I proposed bringing him, it was another situation where they didn't know Ray Carver. I sent his work; they were, I could say, horrified, because they thought they were going to be entertaining this wild alcoholic man from his stories.

I've been writing poetry for 35 years. I have a book of essays, *A Concert of Tenses*. I've written two film scripts. If people want to continue to think of me as the girl from the sticks who happened to be married to Raymond Carver, then I think they're pretty silly. It doesn't matter very much to me, finally, what anybody thinks, because my writing is the main thing, and how the relationship was, how well we lived with each other.

What, if anything, does it mean to you to be a working-class writer, or a writer from the working class?

I think that the more you get able to use language at its highest power, the more you are separated from that place you came from, where people earned their livings by the sweat of their brows. My father was a logger and longshoreman. My brother is a logger, and another brother is a longshoreman. So whether you want it or not, you become an exile from the place and people you started from. I've tried to counter that by going back to live where I was born and be among those people. Ray and I would spend a good deal of our time in Port Angeles, doing the things you do there—seeing the children of the families, going fishing, having meals and holidays together, telling stories, listening to theirs. Ray got a lot of work done there and so did I.

So it has been the place which has nourished me all along, and I go back there with a sense of gratitude and protection and comfort from, probably, the emotional reserves of those people. They don't understand everything I write. But that's as it's going to be, because I'm not going to stop writing the nuclear physics of loss to pretend I can speak only on one level. I think I have poems for all levels.

Are you, right now, what you want to be and where you want to be?

Yes, I would say—with a rage of humility attached. I did the best I could writing out of this material. I have pretty well settled out a lot of the issues after Ray's death. There's one more book I can see I have to write an introduction for. His *No Heroics, Please* is coming out this summer. I've done all I can in a publicity way for *Moon Crossing Bridge* and *Portable Kisses*. I've got some international travel ahead of me. When that settles down, I hope to get to this novel I've had a contract for since 1986. Instead of writing these books, I should by all rights have been writing that, but I did what I thought I had the best energy for, which was the poems, and have no regrets.

I feel good about having come through a lot and am looking forward to seeing what's next.

Jean-Claude Baker

BIOGRAPHER

From *Josephine: The Hungry Heart*

JOSEPHINE'S DEBUT IN BERLIN, DECEMBER, 1925

The city's fevered nightlife offered revues with naked girls and clubs where men dressed as women danced together. The streets were home to young, pretty whores and old, blind ones too. Criminal gangs roamed freely, morphine and cocaine were sold at hot dog stands, and pornographic films were easy to find. Despite its pride in its culture—it boasted three opera houses and a wealth of experimental theater—Berlin was the most decadent city in Europe.

Josephine adored it, and Berlin adored her in return. "It's madness. A triumph," she said. "They carry me on their shoulders. At a big dance, when I walk in, the musicians stop playing, get up and welcome me. Berlin is where I received the greatest number of gifts."

In her memoirs, she reeled them off. "I was given rings with fire as big as an egg; I was given a pair of ancient earrings which belonged to a duchess 150 years ago; I was given pearls like teeth; flowers that came in one day from Italy in moss and baskets …big peaches …perfume in a glass horse. One fur, two furs, three furs, four furs. Bracelets with red stones for my arms, my wrists, my legs."

From *Josephine: The Hungry Heart* by Jean-Claude Baker and Chris Chase, NY: Henry Holt & Co. 1993, p. 124. Used with permission.

J ean-Claude Baker was born in France and, as of 2009, manages the Chez Josephine restaurant in New York City. His connection to St. Louis is his relationship with St. Louis-born entertainer Josephine Baker (1906-1975). He says Baker called him "the 13th of her 12 adopted children," and on that basis he took her name. This controversial claim on her does not change the fact that as her former companion he knew or found out a great deal about Baker, particularly her years in St. Louis, where she was born in poverty and married at 13. She tried hard to forget her St. Louis childhood, going so far as to burn her baby pictures. Jean-Claude Baker worked with celebrity biographer Chris Chase to research and produce *Josephine: The Hungry Heart* (1994), at that time the most detailed biography available. He has published no other books. The interview is preserved here because Baker, accompanied by Jarry Bouillon, one of Josephine Baker's 12 legally adopted children, answered in detail questions about Josephine Baker that only a St. Louisan would ask.

"Josephine Was a Hustler, and So Am I"

First published in *The Riverfront Times,* March 8, 1994.

Jean-Claude Baker is coauthor with Chris Chase of the new biography *Josephine: The Hungry Heart.* Born Jean-Claude Tronville (later, when his mother married, he took the surname Rouzaud) in provincial France in 1944, Baker was a 14-year-old bellhop in a Paris hotel when he met Josephine Baker, who offered to be his "second mother." In 1971 Jean-Claude, by then the wealthy owner of a Berlin nightclub, toured the United States with Josephine Baker, serving as her emcee, supporting act, and road companion; they were later estranged. Josephine died in 1975.

In the '50s and early '60s, Josephine Baker and her fourth husband, bandleader Jo Bouillon, adopted 12 children of diverse racial and national backgrounds, and raised what she called "the Rainbow Tribe" in her chateau, Les Milandes, in the Dordogne. Short on money and hoping to get her unwieldy 600-acre estate to pay for itself, Josephine opened the chateau to tourists and exhibited her children—as a living example of universal brotherhood—to guests who paid extra. Among her legally adopted children was the Finnish-born Jarry Bouillon, a soft-spoken, ice-blond man of about 40 who accompanied Jean-Claude to this interview.

Jean-Claude Baker was never part of the Rainbow Tribe. Nor did Josephine Baker ever officially adopt him; it is more as if he adopted her, assuming his son-ship and her name for reasons that Josephine's blood relatives, and some critics, find tenuous or presumptuous. Nonetheless, upon obtaining U.S. citizenship in 1983, Jean-Claude legally renamed himself Baker and has made a career of his acquaintance with the great St. Louis-born star, a career topped by his book, the fullest and best-researched Baker biography yet written. He currently runs the Chez Josephine restaurant in New York City.

CATHERINE RANKOVIC: *I understand it took you 18 years to write this book.*

JEAN-CLAUDE BAKER: Eighteen years, yes. When I saw the book finished—I'm very proud of it—I said, "My God, 18 years, and that's it?" But it was the most exciting experience of my life—after having lived with Josephine Baker. And why did I do the book? I wanted to know, who was that woman who could be so generous, so wonderful, so complex, so mean, so loving? When I'd been with her, I always sensed a deep sadness, something that had been broken beyond repair. And so I was guessing that if I could find her early years in St. Louis and her years in America—I had to be absolutely sure what happened. I had to find out what it was to be black in St. Louis in 1906, what it was to be raised by a slave grandmother.

You say that what you wanted from doing the book was to come to terms with Josephine. Have you done that?

I don't think so, because she was such a difficult person. One day I wake up and cry because of her, and the next day I wake up and hate her, so when I die I don't know what it will be. But of course I've come much closer to Josephine. And of course you have to try to forgive. Josephine was a Greek tragedy. Her life was beyond and bigger than a human life.

Josephine never legally adopted you. Why do you call yourself her son and take the name "Baker"?

To be honest, because she made me pay for it. All my brothers and sisters were called Bouillon, because legally in France, after her wedding, she was called Josephine Bouillon. But as an entertainer she was Josephine Baker, which I discovered later was the name of her second husband. When I traveled with her, nobody knew that Josephine Baker's children were called Bouillon. My name was Rouzaud. I was never legally adopted by Josephine Baker. I didn't care. I was her son; I didn't care what the name. But when we came to America, at the opening of the Amazon Theater in Los Angeles, she introduced me as "Jean-Claude, the

13th of my 12 adopted children." You might say, what does that mean? But that was Josephine. I never questioned. I loved her blindly. To me, Josephine was like the Virgin Mary.

So the day after the show, a review came out, saying, "Jean-Claude Baker, Josephine's oldest son, was wonderful, and sang," so I was very happy. I ran to her dressing room and said, "Mother, Mother, did you see what they said?" And she said, "My name, Jean-Claude; do you know what it is to have my name? It took me 50 years to make it, and to keep it!" And I was destroyed when she said that. Later I discovered what she was trying to say. She was not upset that they had written "Baker." She was telling us, "Look what I have paid to have that name." None of the children knew Josephine Baker of the St. Louis days. We didn't share the struggle of her life.

After she went back to France, I decided to keep the name, which I thought I deserved. Yes, it is a tribute to her, and she made me pay for it. It's my way to make peace with her. Two of Josephine's children have chosen to take the name Baker as well, which they deserve as much as I do.

You say in the book that you were never a fan. How could you not be a fan? The whole world was her fan.

I'm sorry, I cannot be a fan. She is my mother. The people are fans of Josephine Baker the entertainer. I love Josephine Baker the entertainer, but I'm not a fan of the Josephine I knew privately. Nobody knows the Josephine at home, very simply dressed, with no hair, cleaning, cooking, screaming at us, being a mother; nobody saw that. So for me it would almost be like insulting her, saying that I'm a fan. I'm in love with Josephine our mother. There's something more than to be a fan of hers.

Jarry, how do you feel about that?

BOUILLON: I feel the same. Josephine was our mother and not a star. The mother was very different from the artist.

How do you feel when you watch her films or hear her records today?

BOUILLON: All the time I try to watch movies, or listen to the tapes, because I know the last tapes, but not the first ones. Tapes we have in the restaurant from 1924, I'd never heard them. It's sad we never knew these things, because she kept us out of all that. She never wanted us to see the things and never sang to us.

Once—they say she said, I don't know if it's real—the artist's life was like slavery, and she wanted for us a better kind of life.

BAKER: Josephine Baker was certainly a traumatized child who would need, in the world of today, a shrink. But when you are black in St. Louis in the slums in 1906 there is no shrink. When you become the first sex symbol of Europe in 1924, there is no shrink. So she had to find peace with herself. That's what I'm trying to do in my book, to try to give it to her: "Look at your life. Look at what you've done. How wonderful. There you were wrong; here you were wonderful; there you were ahead of your time."

Perhaps she never knew how great she was.

Absolutely not. Not only did she have to suffer with the discrimination between black and white, but the discrimination among black people. There was the dark-skin black, the brown-skin like Josephine, and the high yellow. For 15 years in St. Louis, where she was married at age 13, Josephine Baker was too light for her own mother, who was very dark. At 15 she leaves St. Louis for New York and *Shuffle Along,* which is a wonderful musical by Sissle and Blake, the first musical written by black performers on Broadway, and there Josephine Baker is too dark for those chorus girls who are the color of Lena Horne, and they are very nasty to her. So what do you want poor Josephine to do? Even among her own people there's discrimination. In Paris, everyone loves her, so why shouldn't she stay where she can go in any shop and try on shoes and hats and be openly admired, 19 and with the world at her feet. She had been deformed by 19 years of America—I'm an American and proud of this country, but nobody's perfect—and when people tell you you are a second-class person and no good, at the end you believe that.

I talked to Josephine Baker's colleagues, ladies who said, "Jean-Claude, we are not proud of what we're going to tell you, but since you are researching a book, we want you to know the truth. When we saw Josephine dancing in front of the Parisian audience at the opening of *La Revue Negre* on October 2, 1924, we said, 'Look at that Josie, doing her nigger routine.' And would you believe it, those French crackers loved it." Josephine was beaten in so many ways that when triumph time came, she could not enjoy it fully, because she was not used to being a fully accepted human being.

Josephine had a rage and an anger, and she didn't know it because she never took the time to ask, "Why am I so bitter?" Because it didn't do to be bitter after all the applause, the champagne, the lovers of both sexes, the cars, the diamonds—what more do you want? She had not made peace with those years in America. It was 19 years which she claimed were the worst of her life.

The years of the sex symbol, when she flaunted with rage her body to the white people, and said, "Here, come get it, have it, pay for it," were her way of getting white people to pay for discrimination. From 1925 to 1940, Josephine was drunk with her own success. When Hitler came, suddenly Josephine was black again, and married to a Jew. She thought that marrying a white man would make her a white woman, accepted by the white world, but she didn't count on Hitler. So, what did she do? She had to leave France. And typically, she couldn't just go simply. She had to go to war like Mata Hari, with her lovers, her diamonds, her monkeys, her dogs. It was fun and it was dangerous; more than once she risked her life. It was a different excitement, a different way to get high.

When the war was over, things were changed. Josephine's body was no longer 19 years old; she was 40. She married Jean Bouillon, who was a great, great musician. After the war, many people blamed the roaring '20s, those crazy years when everybody had fun and nobody thought about tomorrow, and Josephine was a symbol of those years. So what does she do? Josephine's a survivor, a hustler, no longer a naked girl dancing in a skirt of bananas; now she's a lady. She bought a chateau. But she didn't know what she wanted. She could not have children. She could not give birth to children. And she loved children. Or, she didn't love children; she loved herself. She was thinking about the little girl called "Tumpy" in St. Louis. In adopting unwanted children, she was readopting herself, the child of a white man who had abandoned her mother.

In your book you say that her father was white. You're absolutely sure?

Absolutely. No black woman in 1906 otherwise gave birth in a white hospital and had the birth registered by the head of that hospital, except maybe the owner of a funeral home or a minister: rich blacks.

Between the time you met Josephine in 1958 and you emerged with your nightclub in 1970, what happened?

I met Josephine and she said, "Don't be worried, you have no father, but from today you have two mothers." She didn't give a damn for the rules of the world. Who said you need a piece of paper to adopt someone? I loved the daringness of Josephine.

I went to England to learn English, which Josephine said would be the language of the future. That was the best advice she gave me. And then after that I went to Berlin, and after three or four years had my own discotheque and lots of money. A lot. Nobody ever gave me a penny in my life. Since I was 14 years of age I have worked for everything. You can ask my brothers and sisters. Josephine was a hustler, and so am I.

Do you ever regret having met Josephine? Obviously she changed your life forever. And I know she treated you badly, called you a traitor, after you'd been traveling with her as her companion for a year.

I'm very thankful to have met Josephine. The only thing that makes me sad—that's why I felt so empty after she died—is if I'd known the true story of her life, I could have helped her much more. But she never talked about it. We knew nothing of that.

Josephine Baker didn't know what love was. She was afraid of love. I was with her and I was young, successful, good-looking; I didn't even know it. And Josephine never thought she was good-looking.

But she loved mirrors.

But she always said, "Oh, if my skin was whiter. If only I looked like Florence Mills." Josephine could lie to the whole world, but she couldn't lie to herself. And that's why she could never be alone at night.

Josephine was known to be the quintessence of joie de vivre, but deep inside she was a very tormented, complex person. And of course, coming where she came from, her tool, her weapon, was her body. Which she didn't choose, but the audience chose. Her body. So she gave it, she sold it. And at the end, she wasn't very proud of that, so she tried to cover that by suddenly becoming a very respectable old lady who would call herself the Universal Mother.

Jarry, what was it like growing up in a multiracial, multiethnic family?

BOUILLON: I was about 4 or 5 years old when first my parents told us we were adopted, so we had to grow into that idea. But all the time she said, "your brother," "your sister." Just so we wouldn't forget that they were a different color, but that it was our brother or sister. So we grew like a normal family.

Do you remember the days when tourists came to the chateau and paid to see you and the rest of the Rainbow Tribe?

BOUILLON: Yes. We were so young, it seemed like something normal to go to the front of the chateau and people were there, with just a chain between us and them. Sometimes my mother said, "No, I don't want my children to be like a zoo," but not most of the time.

The phrase "Josephine screamed," prefaces maybe 50 sentences in the book. It seems she was angry and irritated much of the time.

BOUILLON: When we were very young, it was easy to take care of six, seven, eight, nine, 10 of us children. When we started to grow—were 12, 13 years old—it was very different. So keeping power over all the children was impossible.

   BAKER: And Josephine would change from one minute to the next. One minute calm, the next an explosion.

What's next? Another book?

Over the past 18 years, looking for Josephine Baker, I met all these old black entertainers, and the passions I discovered about Josephine and her past—they shared that with me. And that will be my next book, a patchwork of early black entertainment in America, from 1901 to 1925. And you know why there was such great black talent in those days? Because they were oppressed people and had to prove themselves. They talked with me very honestly about their professional lives, their sex lives. They gave me pictures, manuscripts, and all that. Unfortunately, most of them are now gone. Thirty-three people in my book are not there anymore. I promised them that I would let them come back to take a last bow to the world.

   Josephine grew up in that world. Those were her teachers and friends. She soaked herself in all that talent. After reading what I think is a courageous and honest book about Josephine Baker, I hope the reader will feel the need to know more about Maude Russell, Johnny Hudgins, Fredi Washington; it could be a good book.

One last question: Do you know how Josephine kept that marvelous figure up to the end of her life? What were her beauty secrets?

   She would weigh herself every day. If she was four or five pounds over—she was very strict with herself—she would take a big glass and squeeze lemon, sugar cane, and water into it, mix it, and drink it. She said the sugar gave strength to the body, the lemon squeezed the pounds away, and the water washed them out. She did not eat until the extra pounds were gone.

Don't forget, in 1935 she had a picture taken of herself using a rowing machine. She was much ahead of her time and Jane Fonda.

The year before she died, in her shows she was wearing a special rubber corset so tight she couldn't breathe, and on top of that a body stocking dyed the color of her skin. So from far away it gave an illusion of even more slimness, like her figure of the '20s.

She loved spaghetti with meat sauce, and beer. She had beer sent in from St. Louis. She was really a daughter of St. Louis, and we're very happy to bring her back.

Carl
Phillips

POET

From *Cortege*

THE COMPASS

a star

dog with torch in its mouth

a finger-ring   but no finger
broken cup   what is lonely
the single breast the beehive resembles
a pair of breasts on a dish

what else
comes in pairs   tongs   forceps
a key crossing a key
the cross but   recumbent or

knocked over
what is called the cross saltire
t
turned on its side

x
that one and
that one and
what stands for

gridiron for the having been roasted alive
a ship's windlass for around
what the intestine   pulled out into
the salt air   was bound fast

what flies   a raven
a winged lion
a winged ox
a man   but with wings

an arrow

what is lovely   an arrow

Cortege, St. Paul: Graywolf Press, 1995. Used with permission.

C arl Phillips was born in 1959 in Everett, Washington. His first book of poems, *In the Blood* (Northeastern University Press, 1992) made it plain that he was Afro-American and gay, traits important to readers and critics then trying—and still trying—to place him in a niche. To Phillips, as he says in this interview, those traits are incidental, and because he is biracial, race in particular has no one meaning.

This interview is notable for being among the earliest interviews of Phillips, given in the summer of 1994 before Phillips became, in record time, one of the most honored contemporary poets. A graduate of Harvard and of Boston University's graduate creative writing program, Phillips in 1993 accepted a dual appointment to teach in Washington University's department of English and in its African and Afro-American Studies Program. Phillips was serving as the university's poet-in-residence at the time of the interview in early summer 1994. By 1996, Phillips was an associate professor of English and director of Washington University's graduate M.F.A. program.

In this interview Phillips refers to the manuscript of his second book by its working title, *The Ransom;* it was published in 1995 as *Cortege* (Graywolf Press), a finalist for both the National Book Critics Circle Award and the Lambda Literary Award in Poetry. The following book, *From the Devotions* (Graywolf, 1998), was again a finalist for the National Book Award in poetry. *Speak Low* (2008) received another nomination.

Books by Phillips published in the year 2000 and after are *Pastoral* (Graywolf, 2000), winner of the Lambda Literary Award; *The Tether* (Farrar, Straus and Giroux, 2001), *Rock Harbor* (2002), a translation of Sophocles' *Philoctetes* (2003), *The Rest of Love: Poems* (2004), a book of essays, *Coin of the Realm: Essays on the Life and Art of Poetry* (2004), *Riding Westward* (2006), and *Quiver of Arrows: Selected Poems* (2007). Phillips has received many prestigious literary awards, including a Guggenheim Fellowship, and is a Chancellor of the American Academy of Arts and Letters. At the time of this interview, though, he was as yet a promising young poet who had published a startlingly good first book.

"People Will Say, 'We Expected Something Different'"

First published in *Visibility,* newsletter of the Washington University African and Afro-American Studies Program, Fall 1994.

CATHERINE RANKOVIC: *What's your background?*

CARL PHILLIPS: I grew up on Air Force bases, so I'm not really from one place. We moved around until I was in high school, and then to Massachusetts, so I sort of feel I'm from there. My father is black; he's from Alabama, which in that time period was not very pleasant to grow up in. My mother is white, from London, and I only mention that because perhaps it explains me, at times.

What do you mean, that explains you? What's to explain?

I think people often feel they can't quite pin me down. Racially, at least, in terms of my poems, people will say, "We expected something different," and I think they mean they expected what they feel is in keeping with a lot of black poetry. One thing I'm trying to do with my courses here [Washington University in St. Louis] is show that I don't think poetry has to be defined as one kind of diction or one type of subject matter. I guess what I mean too is that a lot of the idea of growing up in a black environment is foreign to me, because I grew up where there were just so many people that I took for granted that the world is mixed and everyone gets along. It's made it interesting to come to St. Louis, for example, where that's not always so. Or living in Boston, same thing—there's more racial tension.

You belonged to that special group of Boston poets, the Darkroom Collective.

By the time I joined, two years ago, it was already very successful. There was a reading series I participated in, and we were trying to put together a magazine, *Mule Teeth*, but since then some of the members have gone to teach in writing programs and specifically the two leaders or founders of it, Sharan Strange and Tom Ellis, so it's been scattered around. But when they started, it was just meeting in somebody's living room, and many of them lived together in the same house, and I think there's more of a bond among those original members.

You have a degree from Harvard in classical languages. How did that come about?

In high school, I was going to be a biology major and become a veterinarian. Meanwhile, I was taking Latin. I promised my Latin teachers that I would study Greek for one year in college, and when I went there I found that I hated labs and doing problem sets and all those things you have to do for pre-med, and I was taking Greek and really enjoyed it. I decided to major in Greek and Latin, which at the time seemed totally useless, but I figured I may as well have fun and decide what I wanted to do later. And then I ended up teaching high-school Latin because it seemed the most obvious thing for me to do at the time. I found I liked teaching, and here I am.

Why should anybody study Greek and Latin?

I never had the opportunity to appreciate how complex and exciting the English language can be until I had to start thinking about syntax and grammar in another language. And I think that's what a large part of poetry is, a fascination with language and words and how we put them together. It's true they're dead languages, no one speaks them, but on the other hand, it's language itself that seems worth studying, and those just happen to be two of any others you could choose.

When did you start wanting to be a poet?

I've always wanted to be a poet and wrote poetry from junior high on. In college I worked on the literary magazine, but it didn't seem as if they were receptive to my work, and I didn't really understand the work they were doing. I stopped writing for about nine years and only started writing again about five years ago. Because a lot of writing is so impenetrable—at least, to me it is—it seemed that if I wasn't writing that way I might as well not write, because I must be doing the wrong things.

How did you compose your first book, In the Blood?

It was composed on the living-room floor at the last minute. I wanted to send it off to this competition, so I got a bunch of poems together and figured out which ones I thought were worthy, and then divided them into time periods. And I suddenly saw that this kind of chronicled something. I didn't think it chronicled all the things that Rachel Hadas [judge of the 1991 Northeastern University Press poetry book competition, which Phillips won] says it does. The whole gay aspect of it was actually a surprise to me. I didn't expect that anyone would think that, in reading the poems. But it's fine that it worked out that way, to coincide with my own understanding about that for myself.

Do you have any favorite poems in that book?

I like that "Undressing for Li Po" poem, and sometimes, in a sad way, I like "Blue," because it's honest about my parents and myself. I never really thought about my parents and myself until after the poem was just done. And I like the first poem, "X."

Do you have a second book ready for publication?

Well, it's ready. Whether it's to be published, I don't know. It has a new title, *The Ransom.* It's about the nature of desire, specifically homosexual desire, and if it is possible to find anything approaching happiness or stability for two gay men—for a gay man at all. The lack of overt acceptance of gays and lesbians seems to have imposed a subterranean kind of lifestyle: the bar scene, a lot of abuse and self-abuse, and hurt, so that it seems, at times, as if certain friends of mine are convinced that they're not supposed to be happy in this life. The book is two halves, and it becomes very dark and shows many of the less fortunate aspects of the lifestyle. But then it attempts to see how erotic desire is an element that has to be accepted, whatever your sexuality, and it's just a matter of how you achieve balance, how to temper it enough so that you can emerge alive and respectable and able to respect yourself.

What do you want your poems to accomplish? Do you write them with a goal or a specific audience in mind? Do you write them to raise the consciousness of straight people?

I write them to understand something for myself. If they end up helping someone else in that way, that's fine. I don't feel I'm an activist about anything, but lately I enjoy writing about men as couples, when they're not doing anything particularly unusual. Plenty of poems have the graphic sex and all that, but people seem to forget that two men can be in a relationship and actually go grocery shopping or have normal events in their lives. So a lot of times I'm feeling that I'm just writing a normal poem, it seems pretty normal to me, and everyone will feel as if, oh, that's quite radical, when the only radical thing is that there are two men, and if it were a straight couple they would consider it quite benign and ordinary.

So you don't picture an audience for your poems?

No. Although maybe I should. Many people think I should write more poems that address life as a black American. I guess I feel as if I am a black American and I'm writing about life as I know it, so I am addressing life as a black American. I'm probably not writing for every audience, but I don't know who is, or who can.

How do you like teaching poetry writing?

It's a challenge, because I don't ever think about how to write. I just sit and do it. So it's been odd to try to explain to someone how to get an idea or put it on paper. I'm not always sure that writing can be taught. The most you can do is try to help someone identify his or her strengths and bring them forward.

The teaching of literature is easier for me, because reading literature and trying to figure it out is what I love to do. Not that I couple myself with Dante, but I feel I can bring a perspective as a poet to something like Dante's *Inferno* that maybe scholars of Dante wouldn't be able to, because they haven't actually gone through what it's like to write a poem. Of course, a scholar could bring other things I couldn't. I'm kind of overwhelmed that I can actually teach literature here, that people at Washington University encourage you to do so.

You're teaching a course called "Black and Reluctant" this fall. What's that about?

It's about an issue that's very important to me. It's about the obligations writers do or do not have to address issues of blackness. I'm interested in writers like Robert Hayden, who I gathered wanted to be considered an American writer, or a writer, not specifically a black American writer, and whose poems do not make the race of the writer immediately apparent. Or Gwendolyn Brooks, who for a long time wrote in what some would call a white way, and then in the '60s became much more aware of her blackness and wrote a very different kind of poem. My question is, was she not a black writer before, or should she be considered a black writer only from the 1960s on?

It's an issue that's becoming more relevant today when you're looking at poets like Rita Dove or Ai. A lot of people say they're not really black writers, or they're not black enough. That's something I've been charged with by black writers and black readers. It annoys me, because I don't understand why my contribution can't be considered a contribution to black literature. If anything, it's important not to impose a kind of segregation, or limitations of that sort, and I think the literature is richer for including everyone.

Why would people make it their business to judge which writer is or isn't black enough? There seem to be enough problems in being a writer already.

I don't know. I think about my father's experience of growing up in Alabama in the pre-civil rights era, and I think he feels there should be a voice that speaks of the hurts he had to undergo, and I think that's important, too. I also think there are other hurts, and things just as relevant, that go on in the black community. For example, one thing it's very difficult to be is black and gay. There seems to be a lot of hostility in the black community toward homosexuality. But your question was why people feel that.

If black American history begins with slavery and suffering and continues in many ways to be that, then I suppose people will think that it has to be spoken of. My problem is, I find that white writers—say, white women—some of them write about feminist issues, others don't. I don't feel that those who aren't writing about feminist issues don't care that they're women, or don't agree that there are political issues to be concerned with. But, for whatever reason, they aren't writing about that right now, and yet no one seems to—well, I suppose they do get complaints. In other words, I don't know.

How important is it to identify with your race?

I gather it's supposed to be more important than I think it is for me. The problem in having one parent who's black and one who's white is that the phrase "your race," has no one meaning for me. I think it's as important to identify with being black as it is for me to identify with being white, because I am both. I don't go home and relate only to my father and not my mother. So it's important, but so is the other side. And it's important for me to understand cultures in general. Writing about Li Po was interesting to me, although I've never been to China and don't feel any particular connection with Chinese culture, but there's certain elements that cross all lines. I'm afraid that sounds as if I don't care about my own race, but it's something I never thought about one way or another; it's something other people made me have to think about. In the same way, I don't think of my poems as being particularly black, white, gay, or straight until someone says, "Well, how do you feel about having written these gay poems?" Then I have to think of them in those terms. Makes it interesting.

What's your advice for young poets?

You should write what matters to you, not worry about what people suggest is supposed to matter. And read a hell of a lot of poems, especially not of this century; and from this country, but then from a lot of others.

Donald Finkel

POET

From *A Joyful Noise*

HANDS

The poem makes truth a little more disturbing,
like a good bra, lifts it and holds it out
in both hands. (In some of the flashier stores
there's a model with the hands stitched on, in red or black.)

Lately the world you wed, for want of such hands,
sags in the bed beside you like a tired wife.
For want of such hands, the face of the moon is bored,
the tree does not stretch and yearn, nor the groin tighten.

Devious or frank, in any case,
the poem is calculated to arouse.
Lean back and let its hands play freely on you:
there comes a moment, lifted and aroused,
when the two of you are equally beautiful.

Of the poets in St. Louis, Donald Finkel (1929-2008) was the most loved. Spirited and peppery, eccentric and affectionate, Finkel taught for 30 years in the creative writing program at Washington University, where he was the poet-in-residence and teacher and thesis director for two generations of poets. He indefatigably produced not only short poems but daring book-length poems, sequences, and cycles. His work received one nomination for a National Book Award (1970) and, in the 1980s, two nominations for the National Book Critics Circle Award, the same award with a new name. Donald Finkel the poet is not to be confused with Donald L. Finkel, author of *Teaching With Your Mouth Shut;* Don Finkel the poet was emphatically a talker, whether teaching or not.

By 1994 I had known Don for six years, so this interview turned into a profile, or portrait of the artist, just before and after he retired from teaching and suddenly found himself without a publisher. In the 1980s and early 1990s, presses that published poetry shut down, one after another, including Atheneum, publisher of Don's 11 books, and four books by Don's colleague John N. Morris. Winners of Pulitzer Prizes or other kinds of acclaim were left stranded on the same small playing field with young poets vying to publish a first book. "I think small presses are going to come back," Don predicted, "and they're going to be smaller." He was correct; digital technology would soon streamline the publishing process and allow writers to become their own publishers, which is as small as it gets.

Finkel married poet Constance Urdang in 1956. They had three children. Urdang's final book of poems was *Alternative Lives* (University of Pittsburgh Press, 1990); she also published some fiction. When she died in 1996, Don grieved terribly; and I still regret that she would not be interviewed, even after I had Don pester her for me.

Finkel's book *A Question of Seeing* was published by the University of Arkansas Press in 1998. *Not So the Chairs: Selected and New Poems* was published by Mid-List Press in 2003.

"The River Despair"

First published in *The Riverfront Times,* Oct. 26, 1994

In the winter of 1970, poet Donald Finkel traveled to Antarctica, the icy wasteland at the bottom of the world. Forsaken by all but soldiers and scientists, millions of penguins, and God, it's a place only one poet on earth has ever dared explore. There's a photo of the poet taken there, in front of glacial hills, his image dimmed by flying snow. Finkel's beard was dark then. His parka's flapping open. He's smiling.

Born of that outlandish journey were *Adequate Earth,* a highly acclaimed book-length poem, and *Endurance,* an award-winning "Antarctic idyll." Finkel wrote the poems when he got home to St. Louis, where he was Washington University's poet-in-residence and a professor in the creative writing program. And a New York publisher called Atheneum published the books, of course. Donald Finkel was an Atheneum poet, as every reader knew.

Those were glory days for poetry and poetry publishing, and no one foresaw an end of them. "There was an enormous number of books of poetry being published. There was an enormous number of people writing. They were both going on at once, feeding each other," Finkel remembers. "And this is why people moaned and whined about writing programs, saying they were at fault, they shouldn't be getting all these other people into it. But there were the rest of us, in our madness, saying, 'Come on in, the water's fine!' And the water kept getting finer. There seemed to be places to publish at various levels of respectability or reputation, and it was going along in a pretty terrific way, I thought."

He had reason to think so. From 1964's *Simeon* to 1987's *Selected Shorter Poems*, Atheneum issued a grand total of 11 of Finkel's books—every full-length book he wrote. Honor mounted upon honor as the volumes piled up. No one doubted that Donald Finkel belonged among America's major-league writers. Fluent, exploratory, with a comic edge, his work made art look easy.

Some of his students in the writing program were destined for varying degrees of fame: East St. Louis poet Eugene Redmond; the late, meteoric Arthur Brown; Howard Schwartz; David Clewell, who left the University of Wisconsin to study with Finkel. Although the demands of celebrity consumed some of his fellow writer/professors, "Don," as he is universally known, was always at home to his students, and they in turn adored him. "Bill Gass and Howard Nemerov flashed out more to the world, but Don was the heart and soul of the writing program," Clewell says.

In addition to lengthy and patient tutorials, Finkel gave his students written, line-by-line commentary on their poems—and just plain good vibes. Students and former students could hug him (if he didn't hug them first). They could drink with him (in winter, pepper Stoli was his beverage of choice). He'd howl at funny stories, make his own outrageous jokes, and get misty at tales of hard luck. Invariably clothed in denims, Finkel waggishly sported his trademark skull-shaped belt buckle, and a livid rubber chicken dangled from his key ring. Born in New York City just before the Crash in October 1929, and named Donald because his mother thought nobody could make fun of the name ("and just at about that point they invented Donald Duck," he says), the poet, although graying, still has a young man's trimness and exuberance, and a grin like a friendly devil's. He talks a mile a minute and acts half his age. "He has a lot of energy," says his former Wash. U. officemate, poet Eric Pankey. "I mean, he spins. And his poems are the same way."

In 1988, Finkel had also among his accomplishments and blessings a sturdy marriage to the poet Constance Urdang; three children; a house in University City and a place in Mexico; pets; friends and fans; his health; retirement coming up in 1992 after a full 32 years at Washington University; a forthcoming book of Chinese poetry in translation, titled *A Splintered Mirror* (published by North Point Press in 1991); and a manuscript for a new, twelfth book of his own poems. This one, another in his series of geographical explorations, was at various stages titled *The River Despair, Beyond Despair,* and *Time of My Life.* (The pun on "River Des Peres" is intended; the three-part poem centers on St. Louis' River Des Peres.) Atheneum would publish the book. Of course.

But then, without warning, Atheneum folded. Paramount Publishing, its parent company, jettisoned the highly respected literary imprint to cut costs. And not just Atheneum, but other poetry imprints and presses were getting killed off or were dying as if struck by the plague. Suddenly poetry publishing was too expensive, it was said, even for monster conglomerates; only a few thousand people bought and read books of poetry; poetry always lost money. Finkel's longtime editor at Atheneum, Harry Ford, rejected the River Des Peres manuscript and bade Finkel—and a score of other well-known Atheneum poets and their works—goodbye and good luck. Himself out of a job, Ford went to work at Knopf.

For the first time in 24 years, the famous poet Donald Finkel had no publisher and, thanks to pandemic downsizing, no prospects. He contacted some small presses. Even when they wanted to, none could publish his manuscript. The University of Missouri Press, which Don thought might be especially interested in the book, had discontinued its poetry series and returned the manuscript along with a preprinted postcard: No thanks. A reputation built up over a lifetime didn't matter. It was another, harder to negotiate, kind of wasteland.

"I'd ended up with nothing in print but the book of Chinese translations, since everything's out of print because the whole Atheneum series was trashed. And by trashed, I mean it wasn't remaindered," says Finkel in his tiny gray study, perched at the top of a house near Lafayette Park, where he and Urdang live and work now that their children are grown. "Whatever I didn't buy, whatever any of the other poets didn't buy, simply disappeared from view. Vanished. They were destroyed. I can't say I saw them burning it or shredding it, but it never appeared, and that meant nobody can find where the remainders are. So I just bought a few copies, and that was the end of it.

"At that point I found myself—well, Jesus, you can't go on like that, you have to do something about it. It was such an odd experience; I'd never had it before. Since 1964 I'd been publishing one right after the other, anything I wanted, and suddenly Harry rejects my book and then Atheneum goes under."

What happened? In Finkel's view, it was "a reflection of what was going on in the whole economy. Tremendous expansion. Then the economy started closing down, all the peeling away of unnecessary employees as well as objects to print. They just kept peeling it down. And what would be one of the first things to go? Not the 12-step programs, honey.

"So, poetry, what else? Serious fiction, but that's secondary. Poetry got it, like, right in the puss. Meanwhile, it's harder and harder to run a small press; the universities across the board have been cutting 10 percent. You take that 10 percent off the publishing aspect, we're peeling off poetry. And that's what happened."

In St. Louis literary circles, ominous rumors began to swirl: Don is depressed; Don had a biopsy; Don has cancer. The first two rumors were true, and at that point Don was graying rapidly, making the third rumor easy for some to believe. He didn't broadcast his personal problems; he was the kind who'd mask them with metaphors and merriment. But there were subtle signs: less energy, less of his wicked laughter. And, beneath the glass of his office desktop, he had tucked a piece of paper printed with a favorite quotation, apropos of his situation: "It's not the despair; I can stand the despair. It's the hope."

Now, six years later, a section of the book has been published as *Beyond Despair*, a handsome little chapbook by a St. Louis-based press called Garlic Press. Moreover, last month Finkel got word that the entire book, titled *A Question of Seeing*, would be published in 1997 by the University of Arkansas Press—one of the few remaining publishers of poetry books and itself besieged by manuscripts from other major American poets, including Pulitzer Prize winners, cut adrift by straitened publishers both large and small.

"I wrote to Arkansas' (editor) Miller Williams, because I'd been told that Miller was whining about the fact that this was happening, and I knew him once, about 100 years ago," Finkel says. "He wrote me an interesting note—I don't know if I still have it—that said something really so, so wonderfully sad that I thought I kept it. Yeah, this is it. That, um, 'It was a pleasure to have word of you after all these years, troubled though it was. I'd be a fool not to want a book by Don Finkel on my list'—you're waiting for the 'but,' right?—'but the very dearth of poetry publishers these days has filled our slots with published poetry through 1997.… If you want to take a number and be patient for 30 months, I'd love to have you on board.'"

Finkel accepted the terms, which were scandalous considering that the average time between submission and publication for any other type of book is six months to a year, and considering that by 1997 his River Des Peres manuscript will be nearly 10 years old, with Finkel having long since commenced work on other projects.

Maybe everybody should wise up and stop writing poetry?

"Anybody who can stop," Finkel replies. "Unfortunately, I can't."

Unlike his wife, who is a successful poet and novelist, Finkel feels he could never write prose. So he continues to write poetry, working on a project begun more than 15 years ago: a cycle of poems based on a 200-year-old case study of a child who grew up abandoned and alone in the French woodlands—the Wild Boy of Aveyron. Says Finkel, "I not only decided that I could go now and address myself to long, unpublishable poems, but I could say to myself, 'I don't care about that anymore; I'm not worrying about, I'm not thinking about, publication,' so it's changed my whole attitude toward the way I'm working."

But by the time the Wild Boy book is completed, maybe poetry publishing will again be what it was. Or—far, far more likely—Garlic Press, or another one-person operation, may again rescue contemporary poetry from the obscurity that bottom-line economics has designed for it.

Peter Genovese is Garlic Press's founder, head, owner, sponsor, and distributor, and that's not his day job; he writes plays and teaches full time at St. Louis Community College at Meramec. Genovese credits the formation of the press to his friend David Clewell and to being just plain "middle-age crazy." Genovese first read about Finkel in a newspaper review of *The Garbage Wars* (1970) and realized with delight that Finkel lived here in St. Louis. "But it was 15 years until I met him," says Genovese.

They met socially, eventually inciting Genovese to turn a daydream into reality. The new press was christened Garlic Press in honor of Genovese's Italian background, and Garlic Press's maiden project was David Clewell's chapbook *Lost in the Fire* (1993), followed by Finkel's *Beyond Despair.* Genovese plans to issue one chapbook a year, publishing "name" St. Louis poets until a track record for the press is well established—then later, maybe some unknowns. These good deeds are currently paid for out of a single pocket, and one that's not all that deep. Publishing 600 copies of *Beyond Despair* cost Genovese $1,800, and any money made from sales will fund the publication of a third Garlic Press book. "I think there's a paucity of presses for poetry. This is the only press for poetry here," says Genovese. "That shouldn't be."

"I thought it was total madness on his part, but I understand and sympathize with total madness. And he did it. I think he's an amazing guy," says Finkel of Genovese. "It would seem to me it's an incredible sacrifice financially, and I think he'd like a little time for himself, but he puts himself into it with all his heart, and I said to him, 'It's yours, take it'; I didn't care. So it was really an act of friendship—love."

Genovese took his pick of several manuscripts Finkel offered him. *Beyond Despair* makes poetry out of the River Des Peres' strange history—from a wild river to a temperamental trickle paved over and mostly forgotten—and Genovese, unlike Harry Ford, thought it had appeal beyond the local. "I got my courage up and said, 'Can I do it?' I never thought I could publish anybody of Don's stature," says Genovese.

Beyond Despair was inspired by a channeled, often dry and weedy section of the River Des Peres that Finkel passed daily as he walked the family dog. "I've always been interested in the things that other people turn their heads away from, I guess," says Finkel. "I like rubble, and I've always liked rubble. I like things that are broken and smashed and damaged. I like things that other people tend to reject, and I always want to kind of resurrect them as having an interest of their own. And it was the fact that there was also something left of nature, no matter what civilization, what the city, did to it. It was still there, under this little scrim of dirty ice, so I started looking at what other people call weeds and I call flowers. I didn't know whether I was going to write anything about it, but I sort of smelled something, and so I'm in a sense collecting perceptions and doing research."

The search for the river's recorded history led Finkel to libraries where he found the story of the two French Jesuits who settled on the banks of what came to be called the River of the Fathers, and the journal of Missouri pioneer Moses Austin, written as Austin explored the area in search of money-making lead mines. Using a "collage" technique that is uniquely his, Finkel wove legend, fact, and imagination into a poem that captures the violent contrast between America's past and present.

Critics call Finkel a "poet of place," because his poems often seem to grow out of a fascination with geography—caves, Antarctica, ocean voyages, Vermont, and now the River Des Peres and its explorers. "I don't understand how it happens, and I don't know why," Finkel says, referring to his writing process. "I'll see a place, and I just want to know it better. And the process of knowing it better is the process of exploring it, and the process of exploring it is the process of writing poetry."

Nonetheless, although Finkel is retired and free to do as he likes, the era of his own voyages to the antipodes is over. His future, he said, will be a simple one. "This is where I belong, right here, in this little study," he says. The room is featureless. "Look at it—I'm just surrounded by my desk; I've got all the crap I need right here. On the other hand, when I go somewhere, I sneer at people who think where you live is important. I'm perfectly happy here in St. Louis, for instance. This is a good place to live and a good place to write, and I can't think of any place I'd rather be for that.

"I'll probably just go on the same way. It's like walking toward a horizon. It will always be just as far away, and just as tempting, until I run out of steam, and then I hope I die first before I run out of steam.

"I think maybe small presses are going to come back," Finkel predicts. "And they're going to be smaller. Maybe not as small as Garlic Press, which has its own kind of humor right in its title—it's kind of self-effacing, and I think it's intentional, saying, 'This is fun; this is something we're doing because we love it.' It wasn't as if I was supporting him by my name, or something like that. It was the other way around. I thought, 'Hey, I feel comfortable again.' I'd felt things had gotten out of hand.

"Look what's happening," Finkel continues, turning to local events on the poetry scene, including the recent near-collapse of *River Styx,* a local literary organization with a magazine that over 20 years has earned national respect. "*River Styx* started out, and it was a venture like every other little magazine that I knew was, which is a bunch of people, especially a couple, who have money they're willing to spend. And the editorial board would also be people who weren't getting money for this. They got no thanks or anything else; it was something they wanted to do, and they did it free. River Styx was in a shaky situation because of funding, but the funding was to fund something much better than what they really needed," he says, citing the use of expensive slick paper and dependence on undependable government grants as factors that helped put *River Styx* on the endangered-species list.

What's his advice for would-be survivors of this chilly literary climate?

"Some young guy wrote me a few years ago and asked me, 'What kind of advice would you give a young person today?'" says Finkel. "It sounded like a really soppy thing, but it was a very sweet letter from a young person, and I decided that there was an answer to that question, so I wrote him back.

"I said there's a story in which a new dog is being told about how to deal with a house that he's been taken into, by a dog that has been there for some time and knows the ropes. And he says, 'Rule one, whenever they open the door, go out, because they may not open it again for a long time.'

"I think that's pretty close to what it is, except I didn't know I'd found it out until I saw it there written, it was so perfect, and I realized that's what you learn. You learn to keep your eyes open, and whenever there's a door, go out if it's open, because it may not open again."

Ntozake Shange

POET, PLAYWRIGHT, NOVELIST

From *Ridin' the Moon in Texas: Word Paintings*

WHERE THE HEART IS

i need me a house like that
a small mansion i could see through
from every angle / with one door only
i could enter / i could let my mind
be that / a small castle i could
lock myself in when the world's
too big ferocious and static fulla
things i just cant understand
but my mind is packed with trunks
of memories closets fulla fears /
stairways that lead me to scars
i hate in myself / i need me a
house like that one / a bungalow
by the sea, "where the heart is"
where i can love myself in an empty
space / & maybe fill it with kisses.

Ridin' the Moon in Texas, New York: St. Martin's Press, 1988.
Reprinted with permission.

One of the true iconoclasts in our national literature, Ntozake Shange, born in New Jersey in 1948, spent her formative years in the segregated St. Louis neighborhood called The Ville. A gifted child, she was shuttled to a special school and tormented by its white students. Her Obie-winning play *For Colored Girls Who Have Considered Suicide/When the Rainbow is Enuf* (1975) received Tony, Grammy, and Emmy nominations, toured for years, and is still her most famous and influential work. Her explorations of the complexities and pain of being an African-American girl and woman made her a feminist heroine and brought American poetry to the stage.

All of Shange's works are unconventional. *For Colored Girls* blends dramatic poetry and dance, and Shange, a trained dancer, originated the role of the Lady in Orange. Her writings include plays, books of poetry, three novels, essays, and, most recently, children's books, including *Coretta Scott* (2009) and *We Troubled the Waters* (2009). In the 1990s she published the poetry books *The Love Space Demands* (St. Martin's, 1992) and *I Live in Music* (Stewart, Tabori & Chang, 1994; illustrated by Romare Bearden) and the novel *Liliane: Resurrection of the Daughter* (St. Martin's Press, 1994). She scripted the children's video *Whitewash*, based on a true story about a black schoolgirl who had white paint thrown in her face, and adapted it as a picture book (Walker, 1997) decried as too violent a story for children. In 1998 she published a quirky, lyrical study of African-American foodways called *If I Can Cook You Know God Can* (Beacon). Shange employs nonstandard spelling and punctuation, and once said, "I like the idea that letters dance…"

Shange defies packaging. Her works have been subjected not only to the usual criticism, which tends to find them nonlinear and wanting, but to tests of ideological purity and feminine propriety. Girlhood, daughterhood, and music are constant themes in her work and seem to be acceptable to her critics as long as her depictions are nonviolent and celebratory. A poem from Shange's potent but neglected book, *A Daughter's Geography* (St. Martin's, 1983), was excerpted as the prizewinning children's book *Ellington Was Not a Street* (Simon & Schuster, 2004)—a title probably more appealing to adults than to children.

Shange graduated with honors from Barnard College and received her M.A. in American Studies from the University of Southern California. She won a second Obie in 1981 for her adaptation of Brecht's *Mother Courage and Her Children* and has received many honors and fellowships, including a Guggenheim fellowship.

This interview was done by telephone, because a scheduled interview in person had turned out to be impossible. I do not remember exactly why, nor do I remember how, I persuaded Shange or the magazine to allow me to base the interview on numerology. Yet the unusual interview brought new facets of the subject to light.

"I Haven't Lied Yet"

First published in *Gateway Heritage,* Vol. 16 No. 4, Winter 1995-96.

From ages eight to thirteen, in the late 1950s, Ntozake Shange lived in north St. Louis on Raymond Street, and then Windermere Place, in the thriving black neighborhood called The Ville. "It was a radically defining time in my life," says the acclaimed poet, novelist, and playwright, who was born Paulette Williams in Trenton, New Jersey, and currently lives in Philadelphia.

St. Louis figures prominently in two of Shange's best-known works: her Broadway hit *For Colored Girls Who Have Considered Suicide/When the Rainbow is Enuf* (1975; published in book form in 1976) and the autobiographical novel *Betsey Brown* (1985). Shange has written several books of poems, including *The Love Space Demands* (1992); many plays, including *Boogie Woogie Landscapes* and *Spell #7*; and books of fiction and nonfiction prose. She is currently researching the life of Josephine Baker for her next project, a theater piece about the famous dancer.

Shange's father, Dr. Paul T. Williams, was a surgeon at Homer G. Phillips Hospital; her mother, Eloise, was a psychiatric social worker. They filled their home with books and music, and their friends included Miles Davis, Charlie Parker, and Chuck Berry, who lived next door. Shange attended Clark and Dewey Elementary Schools; she later described her experience of the first days of school desegregation in *Betsey Brown*.

Shange earned her B.A. at Barnard College and her M.A. at the University of Southern California. In 1971 she took the Zulu name Ntozake Shange, which means "she who comes with her own things, she who walks with lions." Professionally, Shange has taught, danced, acted, directed, and as a writer, developed her own uniquely resonant, woman-centered literature. She is one of the most important black female playwrights ever to emerge from the United States.

Shange says, "I still say I'm from St. Louis, and I'm very glad to be claimed by St. Louis. I'm happy to get back there whenever I get a chance."

Because Shange's approach to life and art is intuitive and lyrical, and because she is so often interviewed and asked standard questions, I asked her to do something different: respond to a character analysis (quoted from Ellin Dodge's book *You Are Your Birthday* [Simon & Schuster, 1986]) based on the numerology of her birthday, October 18. She agreed, and she also had more to say about St. Louis.

CATHERINE RANKOVIC: *I'll read you each sentence, and you respond.*
The first sentence is, "You are wild and wonderful, unforgettable, businesslike
and inventive."

NTOZAKE SHANGE: Wild, I might be in certain situations, but I never think of it that way. When I lived in California and taught, I'd do my lectures, then I'd go to dance-class rehearsal, then go home and go over the papers for my class, and at one o'clock I'd get up and go to an after-hours club where there were transvestite dancers, down the street from me. They were really wonderful; a lot of them studied with the same people I studied with. But then when they'd go to these clubs, they'd be remarkable. I'd go home about 3:30 or 4, and get up at 9 to go teach. And I thought it was a perfectly reasonable way to live. And what else? I try to be wonderful. I try to find something lyrical everywhere I go.

"Unforgettable and businesslike."

I can be very businesslike. It doesn't seem like it. It looks like I'm a wandering waif. But I can, because I'll say, "Oh, well, I don't do this." People get mad at me because they don't think I'll do that. I don't talk about money, or I don't talk about my family, or something like that. I do that a lot. But that's primarily to protect myself.

"Your mood swings and your lifestyle are changeable and fast-paced."

I definitely have mood swings, and they do not come with transitions. So they go—I'll go—from really extroverted to being really introspective and not wanting to hear any voices, or hear any sound at all. And I'll want to have all kinds of French meals and stuff, and very elaborate dining situations, and then another day I'll just be in the mood for tuna. So that's true.

"Foreign interests play a major role in your point of view and ambitions."

I don't have a really intense relationship to the idea of nation-states. But I have a very intense idea, or relationship to, language. Language transcends the most boundaries; languages, if we understand them. I like that. To be monolingual is no different than living all your life on the same block.

Some people call you a hemispheric writer.

Well, I try to be. I think it's a misrepresentation of who I am to limit the experience of former slaves to North America. There is no country in the western hemisphere that did not have Africans brought over here by slave traders. So it's a matter of representing all of us, entirely.

"In youth you strain for accomplishments or refuse to be competitive. It's one extreme or the other."

I don't play games. I stopped playing games early on. I really felt murderously committed to winning, and rather than experience that, I stopped playing games with other people. I didn't play tag. No card games. I played a chess game once for 26 hours; I think that was supposed to be my return to game playing. I decided that was not a good idea. And then so, my decision was that I would just compete against myself. I would see if I could do better than before and not involve other people.

"It's one extreme or the other until you come to realize that you have a false sense of values."

That's for a psychologist to discuss.

"In mid-life you meet people and have experiences that demand polished and skilled performance."

That's true. I'm trying to refine my skills, my social skills as well as my performance skills. They're sort of the same at this point! I'm trying to perfect them. Not to make them perfect, but to get them to be cleaner and less arduous looking, and more interesting. I'm constantly shaping them.

"[In mid-life] you change your focus, broaden your philosophy and accept your reality."

Reality—it'd be hard to know. Realities, I would say, more than reality. There's more than one reality.

"Owing to your actions, money and power limit your freedom."

Well, at this point I think I'm marginally recognized, so that doesn't apply to me as much as it would, say, to Angela Davis. There's a place in Washington where no matter how many times people watch me on television, they call me Angela Davis. So that depends, that hasn't happened in a while…. And I really didn't worry about it, because this is my life, not somebody else's.

"An inheritance of money, property, or influence from a male relative is fortunate and burdensome."

I have a lot of photographs my father took, photographs from the thirties, forties, fifties, of my childhood, that need to be archived. Lot of jazz musicians' photographs. I've taken care of them, but I haven't done the archiving. And we also have a house in Trinidad that requires constant maintenance. You have to put roofs on. Anybody who has a house knows about that. Every time there's a storm the drainpipes come off the side of the house. So that makes for constant upkeep.

Is there a spiritual inheritance from your father?

I'm still "Dr. Williams' daughter" in Missouri and New Jersey. I think I've strived all my life to become a person. Not that I don't like my dad, but it'd be nice not to have that name, "Dr. Williams' daughter." And so that's still true. I'll be seventy-five years old and still be "Dr. Williams' daughter."

Did you know you share your birthday with Chuck Berry?

Yes. He was next door to me when I was growing up. A childhood friend of mine now lives in that house. We knew his daughters. Ingrid and Melanie were our playmates. My parents liked his wife a lot. It was just like having any other friends.

"You labor to extend your perceptions to upgrade tastes or products that reach a universal audience or marketplace."

I don't understand.

More or less keeping up with the times.

A lot of reading—yeah. I'm reading a lot of Josephine Baker biographies, getting ready to do a Josephine Baker project. I'm also reading a book on the effects of the Atlantic slave trade.

"If medicine, politics, the arts, or welfare work beckon you, you will expect them to pay off. You are not inclined to live an 'art for art's sake' existence, or to give your talents away."

I believe in picking my battles carefully. When I do work for black people, I do work for battered women and children. I don't think that I'm giving work away.

Really, I think it's part of a struggle in the same way as political agitation is part of a struggle. So I don't think of it as giving work away. On the other hand, I don't think of art as some kind of courtly entertainment that shouldn't be compensated for and respected.

"Organization, efficiency, and executive leadership are part of your character."
Well, I'm self-employed, and I started out producing my own things, so I apparently have a talent for that. I still need assistance. I travel, and I'm not here to keep up with the daily office work. I don't like doing it, but I know it has to be done.

"After your 30th birthday you are inclined to be more liberal."
I had my daughter shortly after that, and I went through a period of, sort of, primal mothering, which taught me to be much less rambunctious and open-minded, I think, for a few years. I might be less tolerant of—ah—intellectual sloppiness. A lot of upstart movements sometimes, they're guilty of that. I don't dismiss anyone simply because they're sort of outrageous; I'd rather have them be there and be outrageous than have everybody thinking they have to believe the same thing.

"However, you are an outspoken critic when emotionally triggered, and plan your arguments after careful investigation, analysis, and logic."
I believe in arguing with facts, not with feelings, because with feelings, somebody can feel more than I can. So if I have an argument, I ask, where's the proof?

People have criticized your work, and you seem to have suffered a great deal, because of your honesty.
That's been…ah, a dilemma, but I've outlived a lot of those people, and I haven't lied yet, so I take some satisfaction in that.

"Engagements, marriages, partnerships, and love do not mix with the loner aspects in your nature."
I've been fighting that all my adult life. I like having partners, and I just—I can be creative in an improvisational situation or theatrical situations. But I do like, I do need, time alone, a significant amount of silence, times of quiet. I've been

trying to learn to work around that. A lot of people can't subsume their personalities to that need. I've got a workspace for myself and keep odd hours, and I have learned to work with that.

"The older you get, the more willing you are to be accommodating."

I'm not sure that's true. That might seem to be true, but I'm not sure that's true. I've learned how to look like I'm accommodating.

"You are more selective, empathetic, and romantic in later years, and have greater success as a spouse."

That's probably true.

"You are destined to contribute to society."

I would hope that was true. I simply wanted to make sure I have contributed to the well-being of women and people of color. That was definitely something I wished to do from my childhood on. It was, that I either stand for something, or I stand for nothing. And I didn't want to die not having stood for something.

While you were in St. Louis, your family introduced you to opera, music, dance, literature, and art. What kinds of cultural things, specifically?

At that time, I studied Langston Hughes, James Baldwin, Margaret Walker. I didn't discover Gwendolyn Brooks until much later; I don't know why that was. Countee Cullen—I knew all the Harlem Renaissance writers. And, let's see, Booker T. Washington I knew about, I could tell you about.

When you lived in St. Louis, your parents associated with Dizzy Gillespie, Charlie Parker, Josephine Baker, Chuck Berry, and Miles Davis. How did your parents meet these artists?

My dad was interested in the arts—my parents were interested in the arts—and they made this obvious. They went to see them perform, met them after the shows, and invited them to the house.

Are there any obvious things that contact with these people taught you?

Accepting the validity of my impulses, I'd say, primarily.

In Betsey Brown, *you wrote a scene where little Betsey is carried and tucked into bed by W.E.B. Du Bois. Did that really happen to you? Do you remember that?*

Oh, that was when I was very young. Very young, because he went to Ghana early in my life. I only have recollections of him from stories from the family. That's the story, but it was only one time, and you have to remember that he didn't like children. That's why she was carried to bed.

How did your years in St. Louis affect you?

It was a radically defining time in my life. My sense of decorum, be it continental or colored, is definitely framed by my experiences there, as well as my inner experiences of jazz, and rhythm and blues, and architecture. Also it gave me the possibilities of multiple horizons, because looking from the river back towards the city, toward Illinois, or towards the south, there are cascades of images that are possible, that can become as real as sweat. At least to me, they became as real as sweat.

The architecture here is special. What did you like about it?

The grandeur of it, the solidity, and the bizarre—I won't say bizarre, I'll say eccentric—but I found in those houses an extended place of wonder. Those interesting interiors, and the many doors, so that one is never trapped; there's always a way out.... I find that back stairways and side doors and side porches are places that many of us had secret raptures in, with young lovers, and memories, and a lot of cities don't have that.

Eddy L. Harris

NONFICTION WRITER

From *Still Life in Harlem*

Harlem is music in the soul of a people, a rhapsody, a torch song, a love song, a child's incantation. Harlem is a lullaby whispered in the long long night, a blues song repeated endlessly and coming from a place so deep in the Blackamerican soul and psyche that the words and the music are somehow known long before you have heard them for the first time, and quite impossible to forget. They are ingrained in the Blackamerican subconscious and part of the Blackamerican idiom. Harlem is the metaphor for black America.

Still Life in Harlem, New York: Henry Holt. 1996. Used with permission.

C arved in stone in the year 2000, the words of writer Eddy L. Harris appear in front of the Emerson Center at the Missouri History Museum in St. Louis:

"The past is...beauty. It is also burden. It is where we go, many of us, to remind ourselves who we are and even sometimes to find out who we are."

A writer of nonfiction, Harris was born in 1956, grew up in St. Louis and its suburbs, and graduated from Stanford University. He tried screenwriting and fiction writing before he wrote and published the first of four critically acclaimed, unconventional first-person narratives. The book *Mississippi Solo* (1988; reissued in paperback in 1993 and 1998) describes a death-defying solo canoe trip down the length of the Mississippi River. In subsequent books, *Native Stranger* (1992) and *South of Haunted Dreams* (1993), Harris told of travels throughout Africa and the Southern U.S.; and a stay in Harlem as a resident observer became *Still Life in Harlem* (Henry Holt, 1996), honored as a *New York Times* Notable Book. All his books explore the politics of territory.

In 1996-97, Harris was a visiting lecturer and writer-in-residence in the African and Afro-American Studies program at Washington University. His work also appeared in *Ain't But a Place: An Anthology of African-American Writings about St. Louis* (Missouri Historical Society Press, 1998). As of 2009, Harris resides in Paris, France, and besides the four books of nonfiction he discusses in this interview, he has published *Jupiter et Moi* (2005), a family memoir available only in French.

"People Pin Their Dreams on You"

This interview was commissioned for a St. Louis periodical in 1996, but appears for the first time here.

Eddy L. Harris, who grew up in St. Louis, is a world traveler and the author of four nonfiction books about his journeys: *Mississippi Solo* (Nick Lyons, 1988), *Native Stranger* (Simon & Schuster, 1992), *South of Haunted Dreams* (Simon & Schuster, 1993), and *Still Life in Harlem* (Henry Holt, 1996). "I didn't know I was black when I was a child," he says. "The neighborhood was all black, or pretty much all black, but it wasn't an issue. We never felt oppressed."

When Harris was 12, his family moved to the suburbs, where Harris attended private schools, sometimes as the lone black student, wanting to be a writer but unsure about the next step. Harris studied screenwriting and earned a B.A. in communications at Stanford University, and then scraped along, jobless, for years, sometimes in Paris, sometimes at home, writing novels no publisher wanted. Despairing, he decided to take a canoe trip, alone, down the full length of the

Mississippi River. His narrative of this remarkable journey became his first book, *Mississippi Solo.*

Harris' second and most controversial book, *Native Stranger,* vividly recounts the discoveries and frustrations of a year he spent traveling in Africa. *South of Haunted Dreams* describes Harris' motorcycle tour through the Southern U.S. and his insights into racism, slavery, his ancestors, and himself. And, drawn by the history and legend of black Harlem, Harris spent two years living there and writing *Still Life in Harlem.* He hopes that a trip he made to Bosnia during the war there will spur some fiction writing.

Harris' work has been compared by *Publishers Weekly* to that of Paul Theroux. Because Harris' books are travel narratives, he, like Theroux, is labeled a travel writer, but Harris demurs: "The journey for me is really an interior one. But I don't think there's a section in the bookstore for interior travels, and you've got to put my books someplace."

CATHERINE RANKOVIC: *So what are you if you're not a travel writer?*

EDDY L. HARRIS: I find my books in lots of different places in different bookstores. And the places that I least like to see them are Travel and African-American Studies. The best place, for my ego, is memoir and essay—it just sounds real cool. I wish bookstores just had a "good writing" section.

The literature section.

That might be presumptuous. But that's where I would hope to be found.

Why don't you want to be in the African-American section?

Because it's so limiting. Nobody goes there except people inclined to it. And it just isn't enough people. I'd like to make a living at this. If my readership is only people who are interested in African-American studies and African issues, then I'm not going to make any money.

You don't find any advantages—?

In being a black writer? Oh, there's plenty of advantages.

Such as?

You get some attention if you're black and you're writing reasonably well and you're writing about the right thing. You get noticed in *The New York Times Book Review.*

The "right thing"?

If I were writing about Frank Sinatra, my blackness wouldn't help. But if I'm writing about Harlem—hmm, black guy goes to Harlem—you know, it's different. So it's advantageous. And I'm trying to take advantage of it as much as possible. That or anything else.

Will you tell us how you started writing?

I had an interest in movies, and it was the movie thing that got me into the writing game. I wanted to be a screenwriter. And screenwriting only because I thought that the easiest path to being a director was to write a great script—and instead of handing it over for money, hand it over for a little bit of money and being allowed to direct the thing. So I wrote all these screenplays and I sent them off to agents, and agents kept telling me, "You write more like a novelist than you do like a screenwriter." I sold some stuff, and I was running around trying to package movies, but it wasn't very rewarding. So I went to Paris to hang out for a while, got a job with a film director there writing for him, but when I wasn't working for him, I was walking along the river writing short stories.

I went back to California and thought I was going to be a short-story writer. Wrote a bunch of stories, sent them out to magazines, and they all came back, with big laughter attached to them—and then I thought, well, okay, I'm not a short-story writer. Maybe I can write novels. So then I started writing novels. Nobody's publishing this stuff. After I wrote about six—six novels!—in a moment of utter discouragement, I decided to kill myself by canoeing down the Mississippi River. And then, kablooey—it's almost as if the writing wasn't going to happen until I canoed down this river.

From the descriptions in Mississippi Solo *of some of the things you ran into, the idea certainly seemed foolhardy in some ways.*

That's putting it mildly.

But you finally scored a hit writing nonfiction. Was that a surprise?

Big surprise. And the next thing too, was not planned. I took the money I made for *Mississippi Solo* to traipse off to Africa. And then some publisher called me up and said, "Hey, are you gonna write about it?" So I said yeah, sure, and then she offered me money. (*Laughs.*) And then the same thing with the next one. It's just one of these things I want to do, and somebody deciding, "Hmm, that's a book; would you like to write about it?"

You were criticized when Native Stranger *came out for not creating a more positive portrait of Africa.*

What can I say? There are a lot of negative things happening in Africa. If I were king of the world, I would set them all straight, but it's a tough place to be. And if black people don't want to know that, it's not my responsibility to lie to them. I'll just write down what I see and what I saw and felt. But I liked Africa a lot.

Did I hear you say, when you were reading an excerpt from Still Life in Harlem, *that you were born in Harlem? Where were you born?*

No, I was born in Indiana and raised in St. Louis. When I say that I was "going back" to Harlem—there's a line in the book that says, "I went back to Harlem, even though I'd never been there before"—I'm just using Harlem as a metaphor. And maybe the whole book: Harlem as metaphor for black America. "I left Harlem when I was 10 years old" means I left being black when I was 10 years old and went out to get a haircut, and some guy told me, "We don't cut black hair in here." Since then I've done everything I could to distance myself from the guys who don't know how to cut black hair—not surrender, not let them have their way. I'm not going to not go to the Metropolitan Opera because it's "not a black thing to do." I'm going to participate, if only to make sure that the white folks don't think that all the good stuff is theirs. So I "left Harlem," I left this black world, when I was 10, 12 years old, and now I'm coming back to it. Coming back to it through Africa, through the South, and back into Harlem. As unblack as I have been, I am still happy to be black. I think being black is a cool, cool thing. Although the same people who criticize *Native Stranger*, and certainly this Harlem book, say, "This guy does not like being black at all; in fact he doesn't like black people, or like himself." Somebody beat up a woman downstairs from my Harlem apartment and I wrote, "This is the end of my being black. I don't want to be black anymore." So somebody's gonna read that line and just have a tar-and-feather session.

How does that make you feel?

It would make me feel great if it translated into book sales. But it seems it does not. In fact, when I go to black bookstores to do events, nobody ever shows up. Sometimes controversy creates sales and makes you popular in some negative kind of way. But in my case it hasn't worked. But I don't care what people say. My job is to write as well as I can and to write as honestly as I can about this interior journey. And I can't write about this interior journey saying something I don't think and I don't feel.

What was your family like?

Weird. I had the easiest, the best childhood that I can imagine. I got the greatest parents you can imagine. I've got the parents who should be running around the country showing other people how to parent. We weren't rich, but my father didn't want us to know we weren't rich, so he always had at least two jobs. We didn't see him a whole lot, but his specter ruled the house. My mother was the last word; she was, she is, a tough, tough cookie. Sweet as can be, and saintly and angelic. But man, she's a tough, tough cookie. They were a perfect combination, almost good cop/bad cop kind of thing. And I think they raised a bunch of neat children. I have a brother and a sister, both older, and it's a very close family.

You've published your fourth book. Yet you have published barely any magazine articles or essays.

I try not to.

Really? Why do you want to do books only?

I'm putting the same amount of energy into the little pieces that I would put into the books, and then by the time I'm done I'm so exhausted, I haven't got energy to write books. So I won't expend energy doing magazine pieces. The last piece I did I had to rewrite five times for some guy. And then you get complaints from the legal department: "Man, you can't say this, people will get mad at us," and I just don't want to be bothered. And it's a bigger payoff if you take the risk for the book than it is for the magazine piece.

You talk a lot about money.

Yeah, I like it. Whoo! Big-time.

But being a writer is one of the least sure ways to make money.

Yeah, that's unfortunately true.

So how do you manage?

Well, as much as I like it, I don't need it, I don't require it. I have managed to do a lot of cool stuff with no money at all. At some point I'm hoping that there's going to be some money in this game. But it's not why I do what I do. The stuff that I do is stuff that I would do for free, whether it's writing books or spending a lot of time in classrooms with little kids and reading to them, or just talking to them, or a lot of silly pro bono work. It's the same with the book thing. If I average out how much time I've spent, I'm making about 12 cents an hour. Yeah, I like money; I have an expensive car, expensive tastes. I like to travel a lot. I like to eat well. Money comes in handy. But I've also learned to do without a lot of all that.

What was the hardest time in your life?

Probably the period before I canoed down the Mississippi River. There were three, four, five years when I was writing a lot and not getting published at all, and being supported by friends and family. I was a burden to everyone I knew. If somebody invited me out for beers, I knew that he was going to buy the beers, or else we're going to sit in the park and look at the trees. But emotionally it was tough, because I'm writing and writing and writing, and you never know if you're ever gonna get around the bend or over the hill.

The race is not always to the swift.

You don't know, so you just keep on plodding. But while you're suffering through your long, slow distances, you are beset by fatigue and emotional exhaustion, and those years before *Mississippi Solo,* I at some point bottomed out, completely miserable. Hence the canoe trip. I cannot think of another period of my life that was lower than that.

What's your favorite book that you have written?

The Harlem one. It sings to me. I guess the other ones sang to me at the time I was writing them. I think *Native Stranger* is the best-written of the first three. But the

South book I like better, because I tried to do more. I don't think I was successful, but I tried. In the original version of the Harlem book, which I scrapped, I was trying to do way more than I was able to.

What sustained you all the time you were writing six hours a day and you're unpublished and you're not getting paid, so you can't pay for anybody's beer?

When I was living in Paris and working for six hours a day, I had no diversion except taking long walks. I have no idea, no idea at all what sustained me. Fear of failure. Maybe an inability to fail. And somewhere along the way I decided that a lot of better writers than I am are running around. But they dropped out. So you could get there by attrition. It's like in tennis. If you can just keep the ball in play one shot longer than the other guy—it doesn't have to be a pretty shot, it just has to get over the net one more time than he can do it—you'll never lose. I think that was playing in the back of my head. And then, after a while, people pin their dreams on you. They want to be a writer, canoe the Mississippi, live in Paris, so if you quit, you're killing your own dreams, but also smothering a piece of their dreams. And I didn't want to do that.

You keep bringing up your old, unpublished novels. Is your ultimate goal to publish novels?

That's what I'd like to be doing. Partly because the fiction lasts longer on the shelves, for one thing. But I also think you can do more with fiction. You don't have to stick to the facts. You can go almost anywhere with it.

What were your novels about?

Eh, just some schlocky stuff. The search for the Holy Grail; a guy who wanted to go kill Qadafi; two brothers and the way they grew up. I didn't know it was schlocky when I was writing it. I thought (*laughs*)—I thought this was great stuff.

But every writer goes through that phase.

Um-hmm. It's practice. Get it out of your system.

Here's a hard question, but I know that you must know the answer:
What is good prose?

It's good prose when it borders on poetry. That, I think, is when it really sings. Good prose takes your ear to another level and makes your ear smile.

Why did you travel to Bosnia?

I was sitting in a cafe in Paris with a purple BMW parked outside. And realized there are two ways you can live. One way is to have your purple BMW and sip coffee in elegant cafes in Paris and ignore the rest of what's going on. But the real other way is to go to the place and really know what's going on. It's to share the suffering somehow. To share the thing, to be a witness to—it sounds really hokey.

What did you see?

I saw what people think of as war, which maybe isn't war, it's terror, because warriors don't shoot civilians, and don't raze people's houses, and don't just lob grenades into the marketplace. That's what the Chetniks were doing waging their terrorist campaign against the Muslims. They cut off the heat, electricity, and water supply. People were suffering. There wasn't much to eat, and, still, people in Sarajevo went to cafes and tried to maintain some sense of normalcy, even while they're smoking five or six packs of cigarettes a day because they're so nervous. They were living in a house that's being blown up because some guy, two kilometers from the front, mortar-shelled holes in the walls. I saw people living through hell.

Why would you want to see that?

Somebody had to see it, and somebody's got to scream about it. Otherwise it's just a thing on the nightly news. I'm not the president; I haven't got the forces of the U.S. at my fingertips. There's nothing I could personally do except to care about it, and go there, and let somebody know that I have seen what they have suffered. My being there maybe means nothing to the rest of the world. But it means a lot to my soul.

And you're eventually going to write about Bosnia in some way?
Yeah.

Well, that's doing something.
Yeah, it's doing something, but the question is, does it matter?

John N. Morris

POET

From *A Schedule of Benefits*

FOR JULIA, IN THE DEEP WATER

The instructor we hire
Because she does not love you
Leads you into deep water,
The deep end
Where the water is darker.
Her open, encouraging arms
That never get nearer
Are merciless for your sake.

You will dream this water always
Where nothing draws nearer.
Wasting your valuable breath
You will scream for your mother—
Only your mother is drowning
Forever in the thin air
Down at the deep end.
She is doing nothing,
She never did anything harder.
And I am beside her.

I am beside her
In this imagination.
We are waiting
Where the water is darker.
You are over your head.
Screaming, you are learning
Your way toward us,
You are learning how
In the helpless water
It is with our skill
We live in what kills us.

A Schedule of Benefits, New York: Atheneum, 1987. Reprinted with permission.

John N. Morris (1931-1997), although he published four books of poems, was the least-known of the poets who taught at Washington University, and he deliberately kept a low profile. He rarely gave readings, was very rarely photographed, and had never been interviewed. I found out only in 2007 that *Poetry* magazine had awarded him its first Frederick Bock Prize in 1981. He was not secretive, only modest to a fault. When he became mortally ill and announced his retirement, I decided to request an interview, which took place in December 1995 in John's office, Duncker Hall 201, in two sittings. I also took black-and-white photographs of John. One was published with the interview in *River Styx*, along with a sampling of his poems.

Because the circumstances were so unusual and pressing—he and his wife were packing up and leaving town—I permitted this subject to edit the interview transcript. He cited *The Paris Review* author interviews as a precedent. John's edits were mild and few. The papers with his handwritten emendations I turned over to Washington University's Olin Library in 1996. I kept the photographs and negatives until 2005, when I reviewed his autobiographical memoir, titled *Then,* published in 2002 by Washington University Press. That review is also a memoir of John Nelson Morris, my favorite professor. Washington University Press published John's *Selected Poems,* with an introduction by Helen Vendler, as a companion volume that same year.

John Morris taught the Spring 1989 graduate poetry workshop, which is where we met. Only at secondhand did I hear how short a time it had been since John had conquered a ruinous alcohol addiction. I never heard him mention it. Cigarette smoking was then still allowed in campus offices and classrooms, and this tall, bony man, always wearing a jacket and tie, smoked like a chimney, blew perfect smoke rings, and was indignant whenever told that smoking was not allowed. I thought it important to photograph him in his office, legendary for its knee-high flammable mess of books and papers, and John's reclining chair. One photograph taken there shows, in the background, a personal computer, installed by the insistent department of English. John never used it, claimed not to know how to switch it on, and wrote on a manual typewriter.

He was working on his autobiography in 1995, having perhaps begun it much earlier, and continued working on it after he retired, in the spring of 1996, to North Carolina. He died before completing it. In it he wrote much about his childhood and nothing about his 30 years of teaching. I heard from his colleagues that he was a talented teller of stories and jokes. What shows in his poems is a gemcutter's craftsmanship, a wit not exactly dry but more like dry wine, and what Helen Vendler called "terrifying candor." That John had a dark side is certain, but I was his student, always greeted and treated as such, and know only what he and his poems told me.

This is the way he wanted to be remembered.

"The Nervousness of the Poetic Life"

First published in *River Styx* #47 (1996).

Poet John N. Morris has built a notable career, starting with poems published in *Poetry* in January, 1956, and culminating in four poetry books: *Green Business* (1970), *The Life Beside This One* (1975), *The Glass Houses* (1980) and *A Schedule of Benefits* (1987), all with Atheneum. On the occasion of his retirement from Washington University in St. Louis, where for 30 years he taught literature and poetry writing, Morris granted *River Styx* the first full-length interview he has ever given, discussing his growth as a poet and what he calls "the nervousness of the poetic life."

Reserved and courtly, a wearer of bow ties and straw hats, Morris is known for wise and tolerant workshop teaching and for poems distinguished by their economy, bridled anguish, and flashes of wit. Born in 1931 to parents who were soon divorced, he grew up in North Carolina and in cities along the Eastern seaboard. After graduating from Hamilton College, Morris served in the Marine Corps in Korea and Japan. He taught English at the University of Delaware (1957-58), San Francisco State (1961-62), and Columbia University, finishing his Ph.D. work there in 1964. His dissertation was published as *Versions of the Self: Studies in English Autobiography* (Basic Books, 1966). Hired by Washington University to teach 18th-century English literature, Morris eventually won a place on its creative writing faculty, completing a now-legendary team that included Howard Nemerov and Donald Finkel.

Morris, father of three, now lives in North Carolina with his wife and is presently writing a memoir, part of which has been published in the *Contemporary Autobiography* series.

CATHERINE RANKOVIC: *How did you get to be a gentleman?*

JOHN N. MORRIS: Well, first we would have to agree that that is actually the case. But I suppose I was born to it. I come from a family that expected its men to be gentlemen. I can remember as a small child complaining to my mother, and wondering why other people could do whatever it was that I wasn't permitted to do, and my mother had to explain that I was a gentleman, that therefore there were certain claims I couldn't make upon the world. It was expected that there might be limitations on my freedom of utterance or conduct. But is it priggish to say that no true gentleman would violate the iron law of genteel reticence by talking about himself as much as it looks like I'm about to do?

Briefly, what kind of family do you come from?

Well, I suppose the simple way is to say, an Old American, prosperous or semi-prosperous, middle- or upper-middle class or bourgeois family with a sense of its own past. A sense of its own continuity. Whole generations of lawyers and farmers and doctors, interlarded with businessmen, an innkeeper or two, schoolteachers, one professional soldier, and in the last century or so a scattering of professors of Greek and Latin and law and German, French, English, geology. Most of us respectable, a few of us interesting, none of us important.

As a child, did you go to boarding schools?

Yes, I went away to a military school when I was 12 years old, and was there for six years. It was called the Augusta Military Academy in Augusta County, Virginia, in the Shenandoah Valley. This was during World War II and I suppose partly I wanted to play soldier. And also where we were living, in the Navy Yard in Portsmouth, Virginia, the town was suddenly full of people, and public schools were overloaded. My going away to school seemed a sensible thing to my mother and stepfather and to me.

What can you say about the military and the formation of your poetry?

Well, people born in 1931, as I was, came to consciousness of the great world in the late '30s, at a time when the world was at war. I found the military world—since I was only playing soldier—a comfortable one. When I was 17 I joined the National Guard. Then in college, the Korean War came along, and I decided to dodge the draft by joining the Marine Corps program, which allowed you to finish college before being commissioned. I gambled the war would be over by the time I finished. I was correct: I graduated in June, and the war was over in July. I then had two years of service as lieutenant in Japan and Korea, with no risk. My point is that the world of the military was a normal piece of American reality, for a male in any case, in the '40s and '50s.

What is the major formative influence on you as a person?

Gosh, that's hard to specify.

Person, place, or thing? Event?

I suppose one could speak of the fact that my mother and father were divorced when I was young, and at a time when that wasn't nearly so usual as it is now. I spent a good deal of my childhood being brought up virtually as an only child. Even though I have two sisters, they are sufficiently younger than I so that in some ways I grew up alone. I was the oldest child on both sides of the family in my generation, and so received a lot of attention. I spent a long time with my maternal grandparents. And a lot of time in the country in North Carolina. Insofar as we're interested in me as a writer of verse, it may matter that I come from a bookish sort of family. None of them literary in the sense of being writers, but all readers. On my father's side, my father was attempting to get a Ph.D. in English, and I probably decided to pursue that as if to do what he didn't quite manage to do. I missed my father. My father had gone mad, though I didn't know that at the time. When I did in later years become aware of it, that was always a sort of interesting fact. And I suppose it was not exactly a worrisome fact, but sort of a dramatic fact. Perhaps even glamorous? He eventually recovered, but I never saw much of him except in the summer I spent with him in 1945 in a boarding house in Savannah.

Does anyone know what the nature of that madness was?

I'm not quite sure what it was; some sort of delusional madness. I seem to remember being told that he fancied that he had committed a murder, which he wished to confess to. Of course he'd done no such thing. That eventually passed over, but then there were recurrences of similar episodes.

That must have been very frightening.

For him, certainly—the unhappy young man. I wasn't aware of it. My mother and I were up north, and my father was in Washington working in the Library of Congress on some sort of graduate work, when this episode overwhelmed him. I never saw him through a spate of his mania, or at least I don't remember. He was always ever afterward nervous about its effect on his children. When I had neurotic difficulties of my own, and was psychoanalyzed for a couple of years, he worried about that. And of his several children by his third marriage, one was mad, and has been locked away for, now, 30 years. Again, exactly what the nature of that illness is, I'm not sure. My father had the best treatment in the world. No whips and scorpions, anyhow, though the usual regime of straitjacket and padded cell was in force for a time. He was at St. Elizabeth's Hospital, where eventually Ezra Pound was locked up. And there was a Dr. White who was at that time the best thought-of such medico in the country. But there wasn't much Dr. White could do about it. My father was one of those lucky ones who just got well, or at least relatively.

How did you begin to write poems?

Well, my mother used to remember that when I was two or two and a half, and could barely speak—when we were living in Charlottesville, and my father was a graduate student at the University of Virginia—I used to say, "Mother, take a song," and I would dictate three or four lines of verse. Luckily, none of these artifacts survive. I don't know where I got that notion. That ceased. And I don't remember ever attempting it again until I was in college, when in Freshman English for a couple of weeks we read Shakespeare's sonnets, and the professor said to us, now, class, go and do likewise. So we all went and didn't do likewise, but in any event I managed to write a sonnet, and I discovered that it was immensely difficult, and somehow very gratifying to do, however badly. And that encouraged me. I think I had known for a long time that I would want to do something in the way of writing, but I had no clearly formed or even unclearly formed particular ambitions. But it seemed—and in my family it was felt to be—a perfectly respectable and in some ways sort of obvious kind of thing to wish to do. Coming from a bookish family and being much read to, and finding certain kinds of things ravishingly delightful, it's hardly surprising. Then, too, any sort of writing is a way of imposing yourself on the world, of courting approval and drawing attention to yourself. It's perhaps an embarrassing fact, but it's so, and it seems to me to be part of a writer's ambitions.

But it takes a long time to develop into a real poet, going from imitating Shakespeare's sonnets to being able to write your own, good poetry. You must have at one point decided to apply yourself strenuously.

Most of the time in college I thought of myself as a writer of stories and eventually, I hoped, of novels, that being the mode of literature I knew best. I had read more fiction than I had poetry. And I wrote one or two stories in college which were pretty good, for a college boy. But the thing I began to notice—this puts it all too schematically—was that I had great difficulty with certain aspects of stories: getting people in and out of rooms, doing all that dull mechanical stuff, as it seemed to me; and dialogue was impossible. And when you find those things difficult, you begin to say, well, gee, why do this? But what I did find was that at some point in any story I wrote there would be a paragraph which had about it some heightening, perhaps even some slight degree of intensity and eloquence, and it appeared to me—not quite so cold-bloodedly as I now put it—but it did occur to me, why not write the paragraph rather than the whole damned story? And that tended to resolve itself into something like verse. For instance, there's a poem of mine in my first book, the last poem in it, nine or ten lines long, which is really all that's left out of 45 to 50 pages of a novel I was trying to write. I kept taking things out, and taking things out, and taking things out, and that was what was left. And maybe that had been the initiating germ in the first place. In college, I would even go so far as to send poems out to magazines, with no success. I published a few in the undergraduate magazine which were no good at all. And then about the time I finished college, I sent a poem or two to *Poetry* magazine, and got back the kind of note from the editor that says, "Try us again" or something of that sort. Well, that was as good as the Nobel Prize to me, I suppose; in any event, very heartening. But it still wasn't success.

The summer I got out of the Marine Corps, before I started graduate school at Columbia, I suddenly one afternoon wrote a complete poem, and then lo and behold, the next day I wrote a complete poem. Then the next day nothing, and then the third day I wrote a complete poem. And I said, "Gee, this is easy! Nothing to it!" Of course it didn't continue. Nevertheless these were recognizably poems, and I sent them off to *Poetry* magazine, and lo and behold, they were accepted and came out the following January, January of 1956, a special issue of first appearances in the magazine. Elegant company: I was with perhaps James Merrill, Richard Howard, one or two others of that sort. I didn't quite realize at the moment how flattering that was. And I thought I was off and running, but I never managed to place another poem in that magazine again until 13 years later. That was a good place to start publishing, because it assured me, or seemed to assure me, that my work could be taken seriously, which heartened me through a good many rejections by *Poetry* and many other places. I did write a story or two thereafter, but I could see that it was rather dull stuff, not very well managed, whereas the poems seemed to me to be decently—well, not embarrassing. I continued to send them out and gradually get some acceptances in not necessarily very glamorous places, but I was pleased to appear in them to begin with.

So you had no poetry teacher or mentor.

No—certainly not formally. I'd like to remember here one man, however. For two years I taught at the University of Delaware after my M.A. year at Columbia, and at Delaware there was a man now entirely forgotten named Robert Hillyer, who in the '20s and '30s had been thought of as a fairly eminent poet. He'd gotten a Pulitzer Prize in 1934; he'd been in college—he'd gone to Harvard—with E. E. Cummings and John Dos Passos, and indeed he's a figure in one of Dos Passos' early novels, *Three Soldiers* [1921]. He's one of the soldiers. Robert's verse was extremely old-fashioned. He was a programmatic anti-modernist. He wrote in strictly regular forms; he could do any of them. But he was wounded and disappointed by the twentieth century. He thought that poetry had taken a wrong turn, that the world had taken a wrong turn. He hated the very idea of T. S. Eliot. A poetical reactionary. And he had gotten himself in trouble with the poetry world by leading the attack on Ezra Pound at the time of the Bollingen Prize controversy in 1948-49. He had taken a slightly unedifying line on that, rather stirring up the Philistines. I mean, he had various disappointments in life. He had drunk himself out of a good job at Harvard where I think he had been the Boylston Professor. In any event, he had taught, I think, as the head of Freshman English at Harvard, where he also taught poetry writing. He taught Howard Nemerov; he taught Richard Wilbur. Indeed, you can see some of Robert in both of those poets. Then he was at Kenyon for a while, which hadn't worked out, and he ended up at Delaware. He was married to a woman rumored to have once been the mistress of Oliver St. John Gogarty, you know, the Buck Mulligan of *Ulysses*. That was the subject of much amusement among us younger instructors.

Robert was a real gent. He dressed in a three-piece suit, wore a straw hat in the summertime, kept a bottle of whiskey in his desk. Anyhow, when I was interviewed for the job at the University of Delaware, the chairman, because I had published those poems in *Poetry*, which was all I had to show on my little letter of application, sent Robert to take me to lunch. I had never heard of Mr. Hillyer—I speak of him as Robert, but I never called him Robert to his face; it was always "Mr. Hillyer." He had looked at the poems and he was willing to be delighted by them, and then he said to me," Have you ever done your finger exercises?" What he meant was writing in rhyme and strict forms. And he quite sensibly said, "Whether you want to do that or not, it's well to know how." When I came to Delaware, he was the only one there with any pretensions to being a writer. And he was encouraging to me, extremely kind. I was at that time beginning to write with some frequency, always working on something. Whenever I'd finish anything, I'd slide a poem under his door, and sometime later in the day I'd go by, or he'd knock on my door, and I'd go into his office and we'd talk a little bit about it. That was very useful. And partly to please him, I did try to write in stricter forms. Some of the poems in my first books which are in quatrains derive from that experience, stem from that. And he put in a good word for me with *The New Yorker,* and I suppose partly through that, I had a poem published there. I remember Robert with great gratitude. I read his poems with pleasure. As I say, it's a shame that he is forgotten.

You were at Columbia in the '50s and San Francisco in the early '60s, times and places of literary ferment.

We didn't know it was the '50s and the '60s. We just thought of it as "now." That's the thing that one forgets. Robert Bly was the first guy to talk about the '60s. He had a magazine called *The Fifties.* It started in about '57, '58; we wondered what he was going to call it next. He just changed it to *The Sixties.* But he was more aware of these things. We were all in our twenties and thirties, that was what mattered, not what decade it was.

Who are some of the other writers you have known and admired?

Well, until I came here [Washington University in St. Louis], I knew practically no writers besides Robert. We didn't have writers at Columbia. The city was full of writers, of course, and many of them did time at the university, but the university took little notice of them. A year or two before I left Columbia, they did bring in Kenneth Koch. He is a charming, amusing, and intelligent man, and I loved the poems. There was nothing that could help me about them, but I admired them. When I came out here, poets seemed to pass through all the time. There were of course Mona Van Duyn, and Don Finkel, and Howard Nemerov, and Eric Pankey, all of whom I admire but whom I don't particularly want to speak of at the moment. Most of the American poets I admire have at one time or another been here. So that's been a pleasure. I don't know many poets well. I'm not much good at keeping up the acquaintanceships that have been established by their transits through St. Louis.

A part of being a writer is being a social butterfly, and you can sacrifice something if you aren't one.

Right. And I haven't been good about that. I don't quite know why. I think I would have done myself some good had I done a little more of that, but for whatever reason, either laziness or persnicketiness of some kind or another, I haven't. In a practical way, I've gotten some good out of the passage of these people through St. Louis. It was Richard Howard who recommended my first book to Atheneum. And on Richard's say-so it was accepted. That was obviously tremendously important to me. Poets that I admire, if that's what you're asking, well, all sorts, but I suppose—it sounds grudging to say that I don't have a great roster of admirations. The canonical modern masters, of course. I worship in that Established Church. Among the more recent illustrious dead, well, Larkin first of all, indeed almost first and last. I find him inexhaustible: the heartbreaking consoler. Bishop. Stevie Smith—that odd case? Edwin Muir, not much known here, I think. Among the living, Donald Justice certainly. William Bronk, do you know his work? He's another odd case: a Wallace Stevens without the airs and graces. Ask me next Tuesday and my list is likely to be different and perhaps much longer. Richard Howard, Anthony Hecht, John Hollander, Mark Strand, all of whose new books I conveniently used to get free from Atheneum. And Merwin—the earlier Merwin, anyway, the magical Merwin; I almost said Merlin. On the whole I seem to take in poetry poem by poem rather than poet by poet. Take someone like James Merrill. I have not yet been able to get on terms with the long master work. But the shorter poems, yes indeed. Works rather than work—something like that? My favorite writers now are William Gaddis and Anthony Powell, but of course they're novelists. And we're supposed to be talking about poetry, which in the last few years I have not been reading as much as I once did. Oh, yes, an Englishwoman named Carol Ann Duffy, do you know her work? I became aware of her only last spring. But I confess in the last few years I have not been reading as much as I used to.

Who are you writing for, when you write a poem?

(*Sigh*) Oh, that's almost impossible. No clearly identified person or even class of persons. Not other poets, at least not principally, although one would hope that the work was pleasing to them. Not necessarily one's family. Some sort of constructed reader who may not exist, some version of that mythical animal, the general reader? Some version of myself? That is to say, myself when I'm not a writer of poems, but a reader thereof—an admirer of poems that are perspicuous, mysteries if need be, but not mystery-mongering, with some relation to common experience. It's hard to answer.

Poems you'd like to read that you'd never found?

I don't formulate it that way, but I think that's some sort of test as I'm writing something: "Would I like to read this?" It's not a sufficient test, certainly, but it's a test.

How do you know when a poem is finished or when it's good?

At this juncture one joins others in taking refuge in that famous utterance of somebody's: that poems are not finished, they are abandoned. Sometimes it's pretty clear that it's finished, and other times you might lose interest or lose whatever impulse carried you through to whatever point you've reached. Telling whether they're good or not is another matter, and I'm still very unsure about that. That uncertainty lends much nervousness to the poetic life—worries about our reputations and so on, i.e., what the hell am I doing in this line of work? Of some poems one is more confident than others.

Is that true of "Hamlet at Sea"? I remember you said that Howard Nemerov particularly prized that poem.

Not so much at first. He once heard me read it, and then he liked it. One that he particularly liked was "The Parson's Tale." And obviously the good opinion of somebody like Howard would affect my response to the poem very strongly. There are others that nobody has ever remarked on, or they have been remarked on, but slightingly, that I nevertheless retain a fondness for. But that could just be a sense of, you know, "What's wrong with my crippled child? I think well of him." Then there are the poems that have been delivered as if by the Muse, and that happens how often, four or five times, five, six times, not very often? And that experience, delightful though it is, such a poem may be good, or may not be all that good. That sort of experience operates surely in the composition of almost every poem at some stage in some detail: a line, a grace of some sort that one hadn't expected that manifests itself suddenly and which may indeed be the salvation of the poem. But the notion that the whole poem that comes as of itself is necessarily better than one that comes by long and slogging labor, the notion that quickness is a test, I don't think is a true one....

There isn't a lot of critical material about your work.
No.

Does that make you happy or sad?
Are those my only choices? One would naturally wish to have had more attention paid to one. Of course, you then have to say it would depend on the nature of the attention.

As you said, "the nervousness of the poetic life."
Indeed. And especially if, like me and like most of us, you are extremely vulnerable to dismissive remarks of one kind or another. Very vulnerable because of how doubtful we all are, or most of us are, and indeed ought to be, about how well we've brought it off, so that a dismissive remark may have more effect than it ought to have. Praise too can have more effect than it should. It seems to me that such virtues as my poems have are sometimes missed because perhaps the poems seem a little more conventional than maybe they are. I have a notion that it's easy enough to dismiss my work as self-consciously minor, as not attempting major tasks. And I can see the justice of that.

Nobody writes self-consciously minor poetry.
No, well—you don't set out to write a minor poem. But you don't necessarily, or some people don't, set out to write major poems. Robert Herrick is Robert Herrick not because he tried to be John Milton and failed. He set himself more limited tasks, in the achievement of which he seems to me as successful as Milton was in his. But the size of the tasks differs and makes a difference in our estimate of the men.

But it's wrong for anyone to say that you were not attempting major tasks?
"Major tasks"—what a phrase! Let me retreat from it. It imputes too much solemn intentionality to the enterprise. I don't think that you necessarily get to choose. I write the poem that proposes itself to me at the moment that I'm composing it. It's true that a Milton decides, as it were in cold blood, to be a major poet, and

designs a life in which to exercise that ambition—but if I had entertained any such ambition, if I had entertained a James Merrill sort of ambition, I would have known ahead of time that I wouldn't be able to sustain that, and so would have turned away from it. What I wanted to do was write as well as I could whatever thing it was that I was then writing, exploiting thereby such degree of talent as I had. The ambition was high. I suppose I'm still not through with the ambition to make whatever object it is that I am assembling as good of its kind as I can contrive. But it's true that what would ordinarily or extraordinarily be conceived of as the larger ambitions I probably did not attempt, unless perfection is an ambition.

I wanted to ask about what you once called the "suburban" content of your poems. You seemed to imply that that was the reason your poems had not been taken as seriously as you would have liked.

I remember my mother reading my poems once, and remarking that they seemed to her the poems of a light-verse poet without a sense of humor. This got my attention, as you can imagine! Under severe cross-examination she modified that daunting view so that I understood her to mean that I wrote on subjects that light-verse poets often write on, but did it, as it were, seriously, perhaps even solemnly, rather than comically. I think there's a lot in that. My mother's initial formulation perhaps resembles, or gives voice to, the view of those who refer to poems of this sort dismissively, as "domestic or "suburban."

So why do you write that way?

It turns out that I have lived a domestic and suburban life.

The judgmental word that people always apply to that is "bourgeois," as in "It's so bourgeois." What's wrong with being bourgeois?

Indeed! Most artists indeed are bourgeois. They are, at least, more likely to come from the middle class than from the upper or lower classes. And one way or another, or sooner or later, they find themselves, like it nor not, living some version, however eccentric it may be, of middle-class life. We are constantly in youth being advised to "write about what you know." If there's any truth in that counsel, then these domestic or suburban poems embody it.

Multiculturalism has taken over in the academy and the arts, which places someone like you, with your background and education, on the margins. What do you think about this?

Well, at my age it's not something that directly and personally affects me. Good luck to everybody—including myself and those like me. We too are a minority.

Everybody's welcome at the table now, except—

Except. That hasn't escaped my notice. Beyond that, I don't have any personal reflections. Those large social questions are so complicated, and my opinions aren't worth more than anybody else's.

You no longer write poems—or you haven't for some time.

I haven't for four or five years.

Is that a natural fallow period, or have you chosen not to write poems?

Oh, it's not a matter of choice. I'd prefer to be doing it. Conceivably the gift has been withdrawn; conceivably I have exploited such materials as were in my possession as fully as I can. I don't give up on it. I don't necessarily suppose that I won't be able to continue. It's true I've embarked on this project of memoir-writing partly because I wasn't writing verse, but there is a slight chicken and egg problem here. The memoir writing may have taken some of the energy that might otherwise have been devoted to verse. Writing a paragraph of the memoir feels to me not all that different from writing a passage of a poem. The immediate gratification and the immediate difficulty is much the same. The exercise of fin-icking skill, the fretful adjustment of words and phrases to get something stated unimprovably or even just adequately—well, it's a moral problem and much the same in prose or verse. It may be that I'm simply taking such inventive energies as I have and applying them in a slightly different direction. A number of my poems are, after all— "memoirist," so to speak. Perhaps there's not a great difference between the enterprises. The memoir business has the advantage that you can get down to it at nine o'clock in the morning, and you're pretty well bound to get a sentence or two by the end of the morning.

How has your life surprised you?

(*Long pause*) That's a facer—I don't know. It's an interesting question, but a very hard one to answer. In some ways, I suppose, one can dramatize it, and say—what is the story by Henry James about the man who thinks something tremendously important is going to happen to him and the important thing turns out to be that nothing happens to him? It's a good story. Sometimes I feel a little like that. Otherwise, my goodness, how well things have turned out! Who would have thought when I was 35 that I would publish four books of poems—and, you know, all the usual pieces of middle-class professional and private good luck that you can't contract for.

Perhaps it's easier if I ask what have been the best and worst things about being a poet.

There are no worst things about it; no bad things at all. The good or the best thing is simply turning out to be a poet at all, with sufficient return from the world to confirm me in my notion that in some way, however small, I have managed to do that. That was certainly unclear when I was 18, when I was 25, when I was 35. However nearly invisible the reputation may be, the books exist and are on the shelf. The better of the poems confirm me to myself. I have put myself on the record, whether anybody notices or not being a secondary consideration. So that early wish to in some degree impose myself on the world has in a small measure been achieved, which not everyone who started as we all start can say. In a worldly way, I have been rewarded for it too, and in the luck of being at this university where they hired me to represent the 18th century, yet were perfectly willing to reward me less for work in the 18th century than for the writing of verse. That is luck not everybody in every English department has. I suppose most of all the continual, ever-renewing psychic reward of actually doing the work, despite the dry spell of the last few years; to work at the memoir, which provides the same, or very similar, experience of gratification, the validation of oneself; and so forth. It's embarrassing, though, to talk about the childish, perpetual wish to see your name in print, because one senses an insufficiency in oneself. There are lots of people who are perfectly content never to see their name in print. They have a sufficient sense of themselves. They don't need to demonstrate to the world—

They do it in other ways, though. They buy the fancy car or biggest diamond ring, or they stake themselves on being the most politically correct. In fact, getting one's name in print is one of the easier things to accomplish.

An insufficient sense of one's own existence that requires you to—

I would say low self-esteem is almost a requirement for any sort of serious accomplishment.

Most sufferers from low self-esteem seem, to me, to have a firm grip on reality! But yes, I know what you mean. A very frail sense of self-esteem, combined with enormous vanity, is the key to the matter. I remember Howard saying to me once, quoting somebody on somebody else, "John, your trouble is, you suffer from unrequited self-love." And that is exactly right, and goes to the heart of the matter.

Gerald Early

ESSAYIST

From *Daughters: On Family and Fatherhood*

"Do I have to buy something, Daddy?" Rosalind asks. "I will if it makes you happy. But I really don't want anything."

"Why? I understand the black kids at school wear Malcolm X shirts and stuff like that. I thought you might want something like that, too."

"No, I don't like that stuff that the black kids wear," Linnet says. "They're these Africa-crazy kids and they hate me. They go around wearing these Mother Africa shirts and stuff like that. They call me and Ros Oreos and everything. But in history class they couldn't even name any countries in Africa when the teacher asked. I was naming bunches and bunches of countries from the stuff I read here at home. But they didn't know anything, yet they want to think they're so black. I don't want anything to do with them or wear anything they wear. I'm black and I'm not ashamed of it. And I don't need a shirt to tell anybody I'm black or to tell anybody I'm not ashamed. All I have to do is live my life the way I want to."

And in a way I was relieved to hear her say this: The commodification of African-American politics and culture, through the low-brow and middle-brow impulses of Afrocentrism, strikes me not as a solution to the problem of black identity, but simply a capitulation to the larger problem of what it means to be an American. For many Americans, it means precisely what one can buy and consume, and an identity, political or otherwise, becomes just another sign of status, a billboard of falsely conceived pride mixed with a hotly induced resentment, not the hard-fought realization of the complexities of consciousness.

"You could just play along with them," I said.

"I don't want to play along with people who don't want to accept me for what I am," Linnet said sharply.

Daughters: On Family and Fatherhood, Reading, Massachusetts: Addison-Wesley, 1994. Used with permission.

Gerald Early's bibliography is a very lengthy one. A specialist in 20th-century American culture studies, awarded many prizes and high honors for his essays and books, he has also been a regular commentator on National Public Radio, served as a consultant on Ken Burns' epic documentary films on baseball and jazz, and has twice been nominated for Grammy awards for liner notes on music collections. He is one of Washington University's star professors, a great public speaker, and an honest, hard-working writer.

A native of Philadelphia, Early, a former paperboy who originally thought he might become a physician, received a bachelor's degree from the University of Pennsylvania in 1974, a master's degree from Cornell University in 1980, and a Ph.D. from Cornell in 1982, all in English literature. He published his first essays in literary journals. In 1986 he made his first appearance in *The Best American Essays* series, that year edited by Elizabeth Hardwick. His first essay collection was *Tuxedo Junction* (Ecco, 1989).

Early joined the Washington University faculty in 1982 as an instructor. In 1990, he became a full professor of English and of African and Afro-American Studies. He served as director and codirector of the American Culture Studies Program from 1991 to 1996 and director of the African and Afro-American Studies Program from 1991 to 1999. You can see that he had his hands full. He hired me as a sort of office assistant in 1991. My job became publicizing the Afro-American Studies program through newsletters and such. I also did research, indexing stories about civil rights published in *The Chicago Defender* from 1945 to 1965. I learned, taught, and helped with Gerald's many non-book projects such as symposia on Miles Davis and Richard Wright. I watched and listened as Gerald turned his interests and discoveries into cultural landmarks; with his scholarship and genius for synthesis, he did no less than build cities of the mind. I read what he published and recommended, and talked over the years to faculty he brought in, including writers Reginald McKnight, Carl Phillips, Kenneth McClane, and Itabari Njeri. This was before nonfiction writing became established, finally, as a creative art worth studying and doing. Gerald Early was among those who made it so.

During the years I worked for Gerald's program, I saw him withstand a lot of flak. It was the price of preserving a great and independent mind. Intellectual pollutants of the time included political correctness and forms of essentialism including popular Afrocentrism ("Black people are Sun People; white people are Ice People," and so on). I left the program in 1997, after Gerald announced that he would step down from the directorship. He went on to direct the university's International Writers' Center, later renamed The Center for Humanities.

In addition to the books mentioned in the interview, Early collected his essays in *The Culture of Bruising* (Ecco, 1994), and wrote the memoir *Daughters* (Addison-Wesley, 1994) and the book *One Nation Under a Groove: Motown and American Culture* (Ecco, 1995). He edited *My Soul's High Song: The Collected Writings of Countee Cullen* (Doubleday, 1991), two volumes of *Speech and Power: The African-American Essay in Its Cultural Context* (Ecco, 1992), *Lure and Loathing: Essays on Race, Identity and the Ambivalence of Assimilation* (Viking-Penguin, 1993), *The Muhammad Ali Reader* (Harper Perennial, 1998), *Body Language: Writers on Sport* (Graywolf, 1998), *Ain't But a Place: An Anthology of African American Writings About St. Louis* (1998), and *Miles Davis and American Culture* (2001), the latter two books published by the

Missouri Historical Society Press. In the next decade followed *The Sammy Davis, Jr. Reader* (2001) and *This Is Where I Came In: Black America in the 1960s* (2003). In 2009 he became the series editor of the *Best African-American Essays* and *Best African-American Fiction* annuals. Early also published a book of poems, mentioned in the interview. He cowrote several other books and edited a pamphlet, now rare, called *Alternatives to Afrocentrism* (Manhattan Institute, 1994), and wrote at least one short historical play, titled *Call Me Out My Name*.

"This City Needs Me"

First published in *Gateway Heritage,* Vol. 17, No. 4, Spring 1997.

At age 45, Gerald Early is a nationally recognized writer and one of St. Louis' most accomplished and controversial intellectual figures; most recently, he won the National Book Critics Circle Award for his essay collection *The Culture of Bruising*. In his essays and books, Early fearlessly probes black history and identity, race relations, and American cultural phenomena ranging from Miss America to Michael Jackson. He is a frequent guest on National Public Radio and, as an expert on black athletes, appeared in the PBS documentary series *Baseball* and in two HBO documentaries, *The Journey of the African-American Athlete* and a special about the boxer Sonny Liston.

A full professor of English and Afro-American Studies with a Ph.D. in English from Cornell, Gerald Early has directed the African and Afro-American Studies program at Washington University for the past six years. Under his leadership, the program has promoted St. Louis as a center of intellectual inquiry, sponsoring innovative public conferences on black Midwestern history, author Richard Wright, black scientists, black-Jewish relations, and the life and legacy of jazz trumpeter Miles Davis. In March 1996, Early was appointed Washington University's Merle Kling Professor of Modern Letters; his predecessor in that position was the celebrated novelist Stanley Elkin.

But at age two, Early was fatherless, living in a cold-water flat in Philadelphia with his two older sisters and widowed mother. "Whenever I would cry, she would always tell me to hush, that crying never solved anything," he wrote in his memoir *Daughters*. Years of struggle followed—to survive, to stay out of the streets, to get through graduate school while being a responsible husband and father of two girls, and to write and publish his first essays. Early, his wife Ida, and their children came to St. Louis in 1982 when he was hired by Washington University as an instructor of Afro-American Studies. In 1986, one of his essays on jazz was selected for the *Best American Essays* series; it was the first in what would become a long and glittering list of literary honors.

In November 1991, Early was stopped and searched by police while waiting for his wife at an upscale shopping center in Frontenac, Missouri, a scandalous incident reported nationwide. "The next two weeks were the most stressful and trying of my life," he wrote, and in *Daughters* he details the effects on himself and his family; he has since put the incident behind him. He is currently at work on a book about a historically black college, Fisk University, located in Nashville.

Early has his critics, particularly fellow African-American intellectuals who wish that he and his essays—published in periodicals such as *Harper's, The Black Scholar, The New York Times Book Review* and *The New Republic*—were more polemical or Afrocentric. By way of response, Early once wrote: "Our profound past of being African, which we must never forget, must be balanced by the complex fate of being American, which we can never deny or, worse, evade." Among other things, he discusses the politics of his work in this interview. In person, in an office walled with books, Early is self-effacing, perhaps a little shy, and he maintains a quiet, even tone of voice except for an occasional ringing laugh. Plainly, he channels most of his fiery intellectual energy into his teaching and writing.

CATHERINE RANKOVIC: *Why do you stay in St. Louis? This is not your hometown. Elsewhere, perhaps, there'd be more opportunity for you as a scholar and writer, and you've had fabulous offers from universities such as M.I.T. Why do you stay in this city?*

GERALD EARLY: I think in part because this city probably needs me, and I probably need it. I've learned a lot about myself from living in this city, and come to a certain level of maturity here. I very much appreciate this city, and I'm thankful. But I also feel in a lot of ways that this city needs me. I probably have become the most visible black intellectual figure in this city, and I think St. Louis needs that visible demonstration of a certain kind of intellect emanating from a black person. Other cities don't need that as much, because other people there can provide it, or it may not be as necessary as it is here. The dynamic of this place is such that, however people may feel about me, this place needs someone like me to be here.

To do what? Stimulate discussion?

To stimulate discussion and to constantly force people, as much as I can, to elevate the level of the discussions that they have.

You said that St. Louis taught you some things.

It taught me about understanding race in ways I hadn't before. I had a certain kind of exposure to it coming from the East, and being out here gave me an entirely different feel about it. So since race is a part of my identity, it just helped me as a person, dealing with stuff I had to deal with out here. And I'm not necessarily referring to the Frontenac incident, which everybody talks about all the time. That was traumatic, but on the whole it was a relatively minor incident in my life. What I'm speaking of is how the whole dynamic of race is played out here in St. Louis, where it has something of a Southern flavor and something of a Midwestern flavor. Then I raised my children here. They were born somewhere else, but they grew up here, so I went through a certain process of maturity as a parent that would have happened anyway, but I was given the set of circumstances I have here, which in some ways was kind of constraining. Because it's constraining in many respects to live here, for a black person. Maybe for everybody.

In what ways?

Socially, I think it's kind of constraining. This town's a kind of conservative place. And people are concerned about certain things which to me seem irrelevant.

Could you give an example?

It's hard to give an example, because I'm talking more about a mood, or just an atmosphere that structures this place.

Is it historical?

Yes, it's historical, because I think it has a lot to do with how St. Louis was settled, the kind of people who ended up running this place, and then with the race dynamic, which is a little bit different than the race dynamic I grew up with in Philadelphia. I think I wound up writing and doing certain kinds of things in defiance of what I felt was a constraining atmosphere here.

You've written extensively about growing up in Philadelphia, but tell us about race as you experienced it there.

Growing up in Philadelphia, I grew up not only among poor and working-class black people, but also among Italians and Italian-Americans. I got to know them very well. Probably one of the reasons why I've never been all that thrilled about Afrocentrism was because I saw the Italian-American version of Afrocentrism. And I just thought—these people are terrifically provincial! In many ways I liked and enjoyed them, but they were just so enclosed, wrapped in this whole little reality—you know, Mario and Salvatore, and the big Catholic church, and this was their reality; and I just thought it was a very narrow view of life. People maybe thought of it as comforting because it had a certain kind of false stability about it, but underneath that so-called stability I thought was a lot of tension and anxiety and anguish and frustration that was masked by this false stability of knowing that your life, in some way, has been laid out for you. That's why I never found Afrocentrism interesting, because it seemed like, "Oh, the ethnicity project again! They want little Africas instead of little Italys! God, I don't want that!" I mean, my temperament, because of the people I was around, just led me not to be interested in that. But I learned a lot about ethnicity in Philadelphia, because white people never struck me as "white people" in Philadelphia. That had no meaning for me. You had Italian Catholics. You had Irish Catholics, very different from Italian Catholics. You had Jews, you had WASPs. They had very different habits. Many of them didn't seem to like each other much. I had to move out here to hear about white people as some kind of collective.

To me, to talk about white people in Philadelphia was a lot like trying to talk about Africans in Africa. In some ways, there ain't no such thing. You've got different kinds of people that maybe together make some kind of construct called "African," but you really can't understand that unless you understand distinct groups. Beyond black people's experience of tremendous brutality and oppression, it was hard for me to understand black people as a unified group, because the lower-class, working-class black people I was around were just totally different from the middle-class black people I got to know. I thought, these chasms and these differences, people tried to mask them over with race or ethnicity. And I felt when I was growing up that I wanted to understand those differences more.

It seems that's what your work as a writer is all about.

I wanted to understand the differences and contradictions in people, because people are fueled by their contradictions. That's what I'm all about. The whole thing with my writing is that I'm not afraid to face the contradictions in myself. That's how I understand what I am, and how I understand what other people are. Whenever I'm writing about black people, whenever I'm trying to write about America, I'm always trying to deal with the contradictions that exist here, because that's how you understand how people live and understand their culture. Because out of the contradictions come the hypocrisies that try to mask the contradictions. And everybody has their hypocrisies, because everybody's got contradictions they're trying to mask.

In a speech you credited James Baldwin with a phrase that you embraced as your ultimate goal: to be a good writer and an honest man. So would you say that your work, and perhaps your success, grow out of that honesty?

I'd say so.

What's the price of being honest?

You get ostracized by some people. You get ignored by some people who don't want to deal with what you're saying. You get tremendously misunderstood. You take enormous risks revealing things about yourself that you know a lot of people are not going to understand. But I believe in living dangerously, to some degree. And also there's a certain amount of risk involved in writing, and you've got to take those risks.

So you're saying criticism doesn't bother you.

I never read it.

You may never read it, but you get other kinds of criticism besides book reviews.

I never read any of my book reviews—my wife does. I get letters here in the office criticizing me about all kinds of things. Sometimes I read them, but very rarely. Because, see, then I'm going to be all tied up in knots about that kind of stuff. I'm going to take it more seriously than I should. It doesn't matter whether people are telling you you're great, or if people are telling you you're awful; none of it, for me, is that useful. I've just got to go on and write, because that's what I'm about: I write.

So it's the same thing with acclaim and success and prizes, you don't take those to heart? You don't enjoy them even a little bit, relaxing on your laurels?

I enjoy it a little bit, but no, I don't relax on my laurels. I'm a driven person in some ways. You get something, and all of a sudden it becomes a burden because then you think, "I've got to live up to it." And so the recognition comes with a price. All I want to do is write good essays, and I want people who know what good essay writing is to say, "He's good." That's all I ever thought about.

You say you're a driven person. What drives you?

Wanting to be good. I want people to say, "He's one of the best at what he does."

What are you most proud of?

I'd say I'm most proud of the fact that up until this point, my kids are among my best friends. I feel very proud of that, and I hope that will always be the case. I get enormous pleasure out of being with my kids as people, and I hope I always will. It's really fulfilled me as a person.

What are you most grateful for?

Being able to write. I feel real lucky about that, real grateful. I thank God I could do that. I think the only other talent I really envy is music; it's the only other thing I probably would have wanted to do, play music. But writing's fine.

What is the biggest misconception about you?

Hmmm. Probably that I'm a neoconservative. I have had several people call me a neoconservative or Uncle Tom, you know. All those things are not true, and in fact, probably my own political beliefs are such that if the public really read my stuff carefully, they would see that my political beliefs are more radical than those of most people. Because I believe that people ought to be free. Most people believe people ought to be enslaved in some way. People are just looking for some kind of way to be enslaved. I believe people should be free. Society doesn't owe you a life. It just owes you opportunities to have choices in your life. The problem is that there are too many busybodies in this world who always want to try to tell you to believe this and believe that, and choose this and do that. And bother you all the time. People should be free and left alone. I think that's the biggest thing, that people misconstrue me politically. But it's hard for them to put me in a camp, because to a Marxist I seem conservative, but to conservatives I seem far too radical. Bill Gass said, "Gerald Early is completely independent," and he's absolutely right. You don't see anybody claiming me for anything. That's because as soon as I say something in one essay that the conservatives like, there'll be another essay and they'll say, "Oh my God, he said that! I don't believe it!" So that's why I'm not in anybody's camp. If I were in somebody's camp, I'd sell a lot more books.

You sound proud of being considered independent.

Oh yeah, I love that. I've never felt comfortable being part of a school, or a camp, or anything like that.

Where does that come from? Why aren't you a joiner or belonger?

I guess it comes from being a kid who more enjoyed watching other people than wanting to be a part of them. I always wanted to be my own self.

If somebody wants to read something you've written, what do you recommend that they start with?

Boy, that's hard; I can't even remember a lot of stuff I've written now. I would say the essay I wrote on watching the Miss America pageant with my children, that was in *Best American Essays* a couple of years ago [1991]. I think on the whole, insofar as the art of my kind of essay writing, I felt that essay did it. I really felt that essay moved along in this seamless sort of way. So I would say that.

You've been in Best American Essays *three times.*

Yeah, yeah. They like me or something.

Where do your ideas for your essays come from? You've written so many. You seem to have a bottomless well of ideas.

Well, anything can be made into an essay if you're willing to examine something deeply. No, anything can be made into an essay if you're willing to examine yourself deeply. What you're doing is plumbing into yourself, and you're trying to make the reader plumb into his or her self. So it's not about providing comfort. After you finish reading an essay of mine, I think in some ways you should feel at least slightly uncomfortable, at least a little unsure, of what you just read. And I think that's what a good essay of a certain type, of a personal type, should do. But anything can be a subject for an essay. I'm not afraid of, at anytime, looking at myself and saying, "I'd like to explore that." So if it seems like a bottomless well, it's because I think any human being, within yourself, you're just sort of bottomless. There's just all kinds of stuff in you.

What are you most worried about? What worries you?
Oh—failing.

In the eyes of whom?
In the eyes of my family, or people who put some kind of trust in me. I think I worry most about that. I don't like to let people down.

Even people from thirty years back, like your fifth- and sixth-grade teacher Mr. King?
He really believed in what I was about. He thought I was going to grow up and be something, so I didn't want to let him down. He meant a lot to me because he opened up the world and taught me to be my own self, which I think is the most valuable thing. I'm deeply indebted to him for that. You need people to believe in you, but you need people to believe in you as your own self. I've learned a lot about that with my kids. You have to let people be what they need to be, and not what you need them to be.

What are you planning for the future? What kind of writing, in particular, after you finish the book you're writing about Fisk University?
I'm going to write a book on African-American culture in the 1950s. And that's going to be, for me, the opus. I hope this is going to be a major book that's going to make people rethink a whole historical and cultural era. And if I'm able to pull that book off, then I'll do what I have wanted to do for a very long time, which is write a book about the history of the church I grew up in. In some ways I feel all the books I've done to this point have just all been training to do that book.

Which church?
I grew up in a black Episcopal church in Philadelphia called St. Mary's.

And you plan to write a history of that particular congregation?
Yes. That's a book that wouldn't have much of an audience, but it's a book I'd like to do, and if I've done these other major books like the one on Fisk and the one

on African-American culture in the 1950s, I kind of feel I've earned the right to be indulged a little bit. And I'm hoping that some publisher will indulge me.

You have written and published some poems too, in the book Daughters *and in a volume called* How the War in the Streets is Won. *Do you continue to write poems?*

Not as much as at a certain point in my life, because I needed to write them. Because they were getting at some things that were in me. And I was reveling in a certain level of being an amateur, and I really liked that. I wanted to go back to a certain kind of way of writing that got totally away from anything professional. It was sort of like, let's say a professional pianist decides on the side that he wants to play a horn. And he doesn't want to go out, necessarily, and bother learning the methodology of this horn. All he wants to do is say, I want to express myself on this horn, so I'm going to just mess around with it, because I like the whole amateur feeling of it. And that's what the poetry writing was about. And it continues to be about exploring something in an amateur way, because I'm not interested in being a professional poet.

You did allow a collection to be published, though.

The poetry is meant to be primitive, in the sense that I'm approaching it as an amateur. But I feel there's a certain amount of real depth of thought in it.

You published your poetry with a small local press, and I haven't seen any reviews.

It doesn't bother me about its not being read. The book serves a certain kind of purpose that's very important to me. As long as I continue to write prose that's going to get me a lot of notice, it's okay. Eventually, probably it will get read, just out of curiosity. So I'm not really worried about readers, because readers come in different ways, immediately and in the long term.

Someone once said, "A writer's life is a dog's life, but it's the only life." Agree or disagree?

I think I would probably agree with that. I think that probably sums it up pretty well.

Kathleen Finneran

MEMOIRIST

From *The Tender Land*

My mother believes she gave birth to an angel. She told me so when I stopped by one day for lunch, and though we have never discussed it, I imagine she told Michael, Mary, and Kelly just as matter-of-factly. "I think there was a reason he was only here for a short time," she said. "I think he was an angel sent to save someone."

My father was sitting across from me at the kitchen table. From merely looking at his face, I can usually tell exactly what he is thinking, especially if anything has been said that either of us might consider questionable. He has communicated silently with me since I was a child, staring at me from across a room or in the rearview mirror of the car until I look up to see what he wants to tell me. It is an unspoken language of astonishment, criticism, and condemnation. It has always kept us close.

The first time my father communicated with me this way I was five. He had picked me up from kindergarten. Usually my mother picked me up, but it was a beautiful fall day, and even though he was still in the construction business, and good weather was a commodity, my father was splendidly care-free sometimes, coming home early and taking us on long drives to undisclosed destinations, special places he wanted to show us. But before we could go to wherever we were going that day, we had to drop off a boy in my class. His mother drove us to school and mine drove us home. When he saw that my father had come instead, the boy ran for the front seat, where I usually sat, so I climbed in back and sat behind my father. As he started the car, my father looked at me in the rearview mirror as if to say he recognized what the boy had done, usurping the seat that should have been mine. When we got to his house, the boy told my father to pull all the way up to the top of the driveway, as close to the front door as he could. "Closer. A little closer," the boy said. It was something my mother did every day without direction, the boy having instructed her the first time we took him home. He hated to walk any farther than he had to. Now the boy sat up high in the front seat to see out past the hood of the car, saying "just a few more feet." My father looked at me in the rearview mirror again. "Here is a real baby," his eyes said. I felt privileged then, and I didn't fight for the front seat later that day, as I usually did when we picked up Michael and Mary from North American Martyrs, the school I would go to the following year when I started first grade. Instead, I stayed in the back to watch in the rearview mirror for anything else my father might want to tell me.

It was almost twenty years later, and many words had passed unspoken between us by the time my mother revealed her belief that my younger brother, Sean, was an angel. It was a few weeks after Sean's death, and she spoke with such certainty and composure that I longed for my father to look at me and let me know what he was thinking. But he kept his eyes cast toward the table and continued to eat his sandwich without the slightest reaction, leaving me to wonder whether my mother's assessment of Sean's life and death was something he had already accepted, maybe even agreed with. He was unwilling to look at me, to meet my eyes in a way that might trivialize my mother's faith. Or perhaps the possibility of what she said consoled him, as it must have consoled my mother. Maybe the trauma of losing their fifteen-year-old son was lessened by believing his life was more than it might have been. Maybe faith has that effect.

The Tender Land: A Family Love Story, New York: Houghton Mifflin, 2000;
Mariner Paperbacks, 2003. Used with permission.

Kathleen Finneran was born in St. Louis in 1957, the third of five children in a family lovingly described in her wonderfully woven and intimate memoir *The Tender Land: A Family Love Story* (Houghton Mifflin, 2000). Finneran attended Catholic schools, then Florissant Junior High and McCluer North High School, graduating in 1976. At Northwestern University and then at Oberlin, she felt unable to concentrate on her studies, returned home, and went to work as a proofreader. Depressive illness ran in the family. It had claimed her maternal grandfather's life and haunted her mother's. On January 9, 1982, without any warning, her brother Sean committed suicide at the age of 15. *The Tender Land* explores this event's context and aftermath and its effects on this close-knit family.

Ultimately Finneran returned to college, attending Florissant Valley Community College for two years and winning a scholarship to Washington University, where her writing talent was encouraged by faculty members Sondra Stang and Stanley Elkin. Stang brought Finneran's work to the attention of an editor at Simon and Schuster, who ten years and three companies later published *The Tender Land* with Houghton Mifflin.

In 1989 she and her older brother Michael visited New York City. "As soon as we arrived in Manhattan, I felt that I belonged there," she said. In 1990, the Missouri Arts Council awarded Finneran $5,000 for her essay "Learning to Read." She used part of her prize "to go to Bennington College in Vermont, where I studied with Philip Lopate. That's where I started the essay that became the first chapter of *The Tender Land.*" Laid off from her job in St. Louis, Finneran moved to New York in 1991. A week after arriving, she was offered a full-time job and a book contract for *The Tender Land.* She worked on weekends at the manuscript of her memoir, completing it in 1999. "People have wondered why it took so long to write," said Finneran in an interview in 2000. "I say, jokingly, that I had to use all the right words!" This eloquent memoir of a St. Louis family's tragedy is still in print and continues to appear on critics' Top Ten lists. On the basis of *The Tender Land,* Finneran in 2001 received the Whiting Writers' Award of $35,000, unaware that she had even been nominated; and in 2003, a Guggenheim fellowship.

Finneran returned to St. Louis in 2002 and began a second book about family life, titled *Motherhood Once Removed: On Being an Aunt.* Her essays have appeared in the anthologies *The Place That Holds Our History, Seeking St. Louis: Voices from a River City,* and *The "M" Word: Writers on Same-Sex Marriage.* For several years a tutor and part-time college and writing workshop instructor, in 2007 she was hired to teach full-time at Washington University. This full-length interview of Kathleen Finneran, from July 2007, is the first on record.

"Acclaim Took Me By Surprise"

CATHERINE RANKOVIC: *How and where did you start writing* The Tender Land?

KATHLEEN FINNERAN: The first year I lived in New York, I would say effectively that I didn't write any of it. I didn't even know how to do it. I was dabbling with it; it was just not working. And then at the end of that year I got an opportunity to get into the MacDowell Colony for the Arts for two months, got a leave of absence from my job and went there, and that's when I really figured out how to do the book. I wrote what became the last chapter of the book there. And by the time I came home from there I really had an idea of what needed to happen for the whole book to come together.

And what year was that?

That was 1992.

So you spent the '90s mostly in New York City.

I moved there at the end of '91, and I moved back to St. Louis in June of 2002.

What made you move back to St. Louis? In New York you were a successful author, and you taught at the Gotham Writers' Workshop.

The last year I was there I taught at the Gotham a few times. After I had been living there about nine years, I was less enamored. I was really feeling more strongly the hardships of living in New York City more than the ecstasies of living in New York City. I knew I would have to make a whole lot more money to ever even live in a one-bedroom apartment. I was tired of living in a cramped space and missing my family more and more. Family members were being born and I was not part of their lives, and that was sad to me. So I started wanting to move back to St. Louis, but in such a way that I wouldn't have to work so much but could write more. A year after *The Tender Land* was published I won the Whiting Writers' Award and got $35,000 with that prize. At the same time a very good friend's mother died and she inherited her house and didn't want to sell it, but she wasn't going to occupy it herself. So she asked me if I could consider living in it rent-free, just paying the utilities. So the combination of that very financially feasible life, along with this pot of money, made it feasible to move back here and not work for a couple of years. And then when that money started to run out, I was fortunate enough to replace it with a Guggenheim fellowship that I won in 2003. When that began to run out I started teaching part-time to supplement the remainder of it.

The book reveals some very intimate things. How did your family respond to The Tender Land?

Well, my siblings received it quite lovingly. My parents initially were horrified by it. As soon as I had the manuscript finished, I gave each of them a copy of it to read. My father was very upset by it—he reads very quickly, he read it practically within twenty-four hours—and so the backlash happened quickly. My mother's a much slower reader, she doesn't really read—my book might be the only book she's ever read—so her dismay with it was slow in coming. But it all came at me in the summer of 1999 before the book was published, and it was so, so—hurtful, and so painful, that I really considered not publishing the book, and my editor basically told me to grow up and decide whether I wanted to be an author or not.

After the book was published, people that my parents knew were reading it and responding to it in positive ways, and then they started to have less opposition to it, and now they think it's the greatest thing out there.

Did it surprise you that the book got so much acclaim?

I never thought of it as getting so much acclaim. It didn't surprise me, really, that it got good reviews, because I thought it was a good book and I was really pleased with the way it came out, so I figured that if it got reviewed the reviews would be generally positive. It hasn't sold very well at all, but that doesn't bother me, except for the way it affects going forward and publishing another book.

But the thing I didn't anticipate was the responses I got from strangers who have read the book who have written me letters or e-mails. That kind of acclaim took me by surprise. And then things happened, like when the paperback came out, and the book was chosen for the Honolulu book club, and chosen for the citywide book club of Sarasota, Florida, and I got to go down there and do a reading. It was really lovely and unexpected.

You do know that The Tender Land is a masterpiece, don't you?

I don't think it's a masterpiece, but I think it's really good.

How are you going to top it?

I don't know that I am, really, and that's been a kind of stumbling block in finishing my next book, this fear that it's never going to match the first one. And I've resigned myself to the fact that it just isn't going to. When I am feeling really dismayed about writing and about my abilities, what I do to overcome it is to just read parts of *The Tender Land,* and it usually always just knocks me out!

Another aspect of having a book out in the world that surprised me, was, there's a writer named Jonathan Franzen, who grew up in Webster Groves. I never knew him personally, but I came to find out he was probably responsible for me winning the Whiting, or at least being nominated for the Whiting, and was very instrumental in my getting a Guggenheim.

Did you know him?

Subsequently I met him, yes, when he was in town a few years ago; he was doing research on one of his essays that ran in *The New Yorker*. And I met him then for the first time. And then recently there was an article that ran in *New York Magazine* at the beginning of June [2007], their summer-reading issue, and they had an article in that issue called "The Best Books You've Never Read." They asked the critics in the National Book Critics Circle to name a book that was published in the past ten years that they felt was underappreciated, and one of the critics at *The Washington Post* named mine. So I sent her an e-mail to thank her. She was surprised to hear from me, and she went on to tell me that she had gotten the book from Jonathan Franzen after it came out. So just finding out that the regard of other writers has been there has been very gratifying.

As an undergraduate, you studied writing at Washington University with Sondra Stang and Stanley Elkin. I have heard that Elkin could be very hard on his students.

He had a reputation for being quite crushing, but I didn't find that to be my experience in our workshop. He was quite charming in his response to people's work. He was really helpful to me along the way. He gave me a recommendation to go to the MacDowell Colony, things like that.

Do you wish you had an M.F.A. degree?

I used to. I stopped wishing that. I guess because I published anyway, I haven't really thought about it much. I did have regrets about it for a while. I was so bad at being in school that I didn't feel like going through that torture again.

Did writing your book help you feel better?

Well, I went on antidepressants in the mid-1990s, so my depression was successfully treated and that probably enabled me to actually finish writing the book.

The sense of accomplishment was a real antidote to depression. Around the same time I finished writing the book, I finished my final credits for my bachelor's degree, so there was a concentrated period of time where everything seemed to complete itself, and that was a large boost.

Do you want to say anything about being a woman writer?
I've never given a moment's thought to it.

Why not?
I don't know.

Why did you return to St. Louis? What is it you like about it?
What I like most about St. Louis, I think, is its familiarity to me and how different parts of it have meaning for me in relation to different parts of my life. Since I've returned from New York, I also appreciate being able to count myself among a community of writers.

Why do you think the writing and reading of memoirs is so popular now?
(*Long pause*) Maybe—sadly—it might have to do with fewer people in the world being real readers and not having the gifts of a reading imagination. People want to find someone whose lives look in some regard like theirs. I find that a lot of readers of my memoir seem to appreciate that aspect of the memoir. That kind of leads me toward setting the record straight on misperceptions about me. One of the things that bothers me is that people assume that I'm not a writer, when in fact I wrote this memoir because I am a writer. I had this story to tell about my brother, but I wrote that story because I am a writer. I think writers who haven't published fiction before they've published a memoir get strapped as someone who has a story to tell as opposed to being a writer who chose to write about that story.

Are there any other misperceptions about you?
None I care to mention.

Are you going to try writing fiction?
I would really love to, but I have no imagination.

But how can you say that?

Because I know. I've been trying to think of stories that have no basis in my life. I never can.

What is it you have if you don't have imagination?

I have a good instinct about how to tell a story. I think I have a really good ear for language and the poetry of prose.

What are your thoughts about writing and money?

The money disturbs me in the sense that so much of the money in the publishing world is going to celebrities who are writing their celebrity bios or who are writing novels or memoirs. Whether they have literary value or not—and I'm sure some of them do have literary value—but the literary value of them is not any greater than that of a writer's. And I think all the millions of dollars going toward these celebrity-based books, so much of that could be funding real books by real writers. It's so disheartening, but that's just part of the whole celebrity chaos that America has become.

What writing schedule or routine is most productive for you?

When I was writing *The Tender Land* I tried to write every night when I got home after work, and after about a year and a half I couldn't sustain that anymore, because when you're really involved in a piece of writing it's hard to turn your brain off and go to sleep, and then I'd be a disaster the next day at work. So I denied myself the opportunity to write during the week, I didn't let myself write during the week, and only wrote on weekends. And by doing that I sort of imagined myself going to writer's camp in my apartment every weekend, where it was really a luxurious schedule. It worked pretty well. Now my employment is teaching, and so usually I can work out a schedule where I have either two days or three days on. So if I have a Monday-Wednesday-Friday teaching schedule, I have Tuesdays and Thursdays to write. While I'm writing I tend to need large blocks of time. That could be one- or two-hour blocks, but usually I like six to eight hours, because I want to really be able to settle into it and be there for a while. I write by hand. I write longhand and then when I have about 20 pages, I transfer it onto a computer file and do a second draft out of all the typed copy.

Do you think you had to leave St. Louis to write about it?

Well, I didn't think that I did. But I see in retrospect that I never, ever, ever would have been able to write *The Tender Land* living in the presence of my family. Having the luxury of distance enriched the sort of objectivity you need to do memoir writing well.

Qiu Xiaolong

POET AND NOVELIST

From *Don Quixote in China*

4

        At the entrance
of a village, an old woman
stands still, almost statuesque
in her small bound feet, hawking
popsicles from a ramshackle wheelbarrow,
her face as weather-beaten
as a Qing terra-cotta figurine
on a postcard. White towel-hooded,
she is swathed in black homespun,
impervious, like a piece of glass
smoke-darkened to watch
an eclipse of the summer sun. There
are occasionally rustlings
of a few leaves when a cicada starts
chirping. From a makeshift
freezer of a cotton-padded overcoat,
she is producing a miracle
to an old villager on a stretcher,
who, dying, is finally tasting,
for the first time, the frozen taste
of his dream. She places the popsicle
in his hands, as if in sublimation
of her own lifelong pursuit.
A smile falls into the tin,
mingled with the coins—as solemn,
satisfied. A horsefly hums

in suspicion. She must have come
from an aristocratic Manchurian family:
the wooden wheel bears an emblem
of Golden Water Bridge.
A princess, perhaps, driven
out of the distant pagoda.
You are declaring your heroic campaign
for her salvation when she jabbed
the wheelbarrow into your ribs. "After
thirty years, I have finally won
the right to be a member
of the laboring people. It is your brain
that needs washing." A badge of
Best Socialist Mobile Service Woman
in Chairman Mao's calligraphy
shining magically on her shrunken bosom.
A lanky shadow—you wonder
whether it's yours—starts turning
into a plastic stick feeling
a colored slab of time melting
to its own satisfaction. Nothing
left on the wheelbarrow,
she wheels nothing back
into the dusk.

Qiu Xiaolong's mystery novels featuring the Shanghai detective Inspector Chen are bestsellers worldwide and have been translated into 10 languages. Born in Shanghai in 1953, Qiu first came to the U.S. in 1988 as a Ford Foundation Fellow attending Washington University's graduate program in poetry. He was already a prominent Chinese poet and poetry translator: His translations of T.S. Eliot and other Modernists changed the direction of contemporary Chinese poetry. Horrified by the massacre of protestors, mostly students, at Tiananmen Square in Beijing in 1989, Qiu was fingered by the Chinese government as a supporter of the protestors—he'd been seen frying spring rolls at a St. Louis fundraiser—and became an instant exile. He remained in the U.S., settling in St. Louis, T.S. Eliot's hometown. He and his wife, Wang Lijun, had daughter Julia in 1990.

Great political events have formed and shaken him, and they permeate his writings. In 1966, young Qiu, bedridden with bronchitis, was spared the "re-education" that Mao's Cultural Revolution forced on China's middle class. While his peers were sent a thousand miles from home to do manual labor, Qiu was able to stay in school. His father, who before 1949 owned a perfume company, was publicly humiliated as an exploiter of the working class; Qiu wrote his father's public self-denunciation because his father was too sick to compose it himself. Inspired by the sight of an English-language textbook, Qiu eventually earned a degree in English from East China Normal University. Although admitted to the Chinese Writers Association, he never became a "professional writer" in Chinese terms; that is, salaried by the government. "A disadvantage of that is that you may not write freely," Qiu said, "but even if you were not a member, you could not write that freely." The government could well have assigned Qiu a job in public works or law enforcement; that's how Qiu's fictional detective hero, Inspector Chen, a poet at heart, got his position.

Qiu had important friendships with poet-critic M.L. Rosenthal and the St. Louis literary couple Jarvis Thurston and Mona Van Duyn, U.S. Poet Laureate in 1992-93. Qiu helped his teacher Donald Finkel translate into English selected works by contemporary Chinese poets. As Qiu wrote and published more poetry in English, his star began to rise. His first novel, *Death of a Red Heroine*, a story of corruption and crime in modern Shanghai, was published in 2000. In 2006 *The Wall Street Journal* named it one of the "five best political novels of all time." Inspector Chen mystery novels now include *A Loyal Character Dancer, When Red is Black, A Case of Two Cities, Red Mandarin Dress,* and *The Mao Case.* A newer book of short stories, described here, created a stir. He often travels overseas to meet editors, booksellers, and fans, and to research China's changing culture. His novels are published in China, but only after strict editorial "haircuts."

I met Qiu in a classroom, just after he arrived in the U.S. He had none of the dishy, dashing quality he has now. On the fire escape outside his apartment on Heman Street, Qiu, his wife, and I dined on barbecued pork (he is a fine cook). When he went fishing he brought me selections from his catch. I brought him an entry form for the 1994 Missouri Arts Council's biennial literary contest, its prize $5,000. He sent in his poetry and won.

For the next several years Qiu studied for his doctorate in comparative literature, operated the East-West Translation Service, and continued to write in English. He now writes fiction full time. He has taught language and literature at Washington University and at St. Louis Community College. The interview below was done in March 2009.

Qiu's name is pronounced "Cho Shaw-long." Qiu is his family name; "Xiaolong" means "little dragon."

"Things You Can Call Universal"

CATHERINE RANKOVIC: *I heard that you were mentioned on a sex program in China. What's that all about?*

QIU XIAOLONG: If you google that, you can watch the video clip. It seems to be quite popular. I think the whole series is called *Sexy Beijing* or something.

So you are a sex symbol there.

No, no, no, nothing to do with me. They just interviewed me in a park. They did not even tell me the name of that particular program. In the video clip you can see the producer, actually the producer herself, in her underwear, reading my book. That, I did not know until someone told me. I was like, "What?"

Do your books sell well in China?

Not too bad, but not a lot in China.

Where do your books sell best?

I think in France and Germany.

From what I understand, your book of poems, Lines Around China, *has been reissued. That must mean the book is in demand.*

I think so, because I got e-mails from readers asking where to buy the book. I told them, but I hardly got any response from the publisher. About the publishing business I have no clue. They changed the cover. I don't hear from them. That's okay, as long as the poetry book is out. If people enjoy reading that, I'm happy.

How are your wife and daughter?

Oh, they do fine. Julia's in college already.

You once said that you worked for her, that your real job was to chauffeur her to all her activities.

I still work for her. I have to provide for her. Nowadays college is very expensive. And she's a big spender.

Is she?

(*Smile and sigh.*) It's okay. I still work for her.

You have an international reputation as a mystery writer. But that's not all you do.

I write mysteries, no question about that, but I don't want to be confined to that particular conception. I write poetry, I write short stories, and my collection of linked stories—*Years of Red Dust*—was serialized in *Le Monde*. And that collection will also come out in Germany, in Italy, and in English, soon, I hope.

Is there a reason it appeared in France first? Why not the United States first?

Because *Le Monde* demanded it. But it's not a project I did just for that newspaper. I was working on it for a long time before that. They had a deadline because the original is in English, and they had to translate it into French. But even after I gave them the manuscript I was not really happy, because it was a rush-rush job. I wanted to work on the English text again. So I did not give my publisher the English text until half a year later. I don't want to give something out not polished.

And what was the response to the serialization in Le Monde?

The response went really well. Some readers told me they didn't normally read stories, but these stories about China happened to be printed about the same time as the Olympics in Beijing, and they were really happy about that. Also I got some responses from editors and critics. They were quite happy, too, saying, "Wow, that shows that you are not just a mystery writer."

Since it's a creative departure for you, will you talk a bit about Years of Red Dust?

"Red Dust" is the name of a lane, like a neighborhood, in Shanghai. The stories are structured around the people living in that lane. And in Shanghai, people used to—people still do, sometimes—sit outside in the evening and tell stories. People in the 1960s and '70s did not have air conditioning in their homes; some did not even have electric fans. So people sat out a lot, and they mixed a lot, and they told stories. So these stories are narrated by people in the lane, about what's happening in the lane, or at least related to it.

There's one thing about the stories I think is experimental for me. In Shanghai neighborhoods even today, you can see a blackboard newsletter. Not everyone can, or wants to, read a newspaper, but the government still wants to do propaganda work, writing what a great job they have done for the year. So there's this kind of blackboard newsletter. At the beginning of each story I put one blackboard newsletter that summarizes the political events of the year; it could be 1957 or 1961. The contents of the newsletter may have something to do with the story. Of course everything is much the same everywhere, but in China things can be more political than anywhere else. When people in the lane tell a story, they tell it from the political or social perspective of that time, so a story with a lot of meaning in the '60s suddenly goes to the opposite, or becomes ironical. The collection is maybe 26 or 27 stories so far. I probably will write another collection for those years not covered (*laugh*) in the first collection. I will do that. It's very interesting to me. A German documentary producer wants me to go to Shanghai to talk about those stories in front of that lane, because that lane is based on a real lane. That will be fun, as long as I am not arrested by the neighborhood police.

You think that would happen?

It is true that China has changed a lot, but that particular neighborhood has not. A lot of people would like me to show off the new mansions, the luxurious hotel, but if I show a neighborhood kind of left out, they would not be happy. But that neighborhood is not something I created in fiction. It's based on real life, so I don't see anything wrong with that. Actually there are a lot of neighborhoods still like that.

Is that your old neighborhood?

Very close to my old neighborhood. I used to have a lot of friends and schoolmates in that particular lane, so I was familiar with the layout, with the life.

You're a very productive writer.

(*Laughs.*) I have to work for my daughter, yes.

How do you manage to issue a novel every year and a half, and other books besides?

Partially I must credit the publishers. They are always behind you. They say, "When can you give us a manuscript?" I think I'm a quite lazy man. But sometimes I purposely give a deadline to myself by promising to give the publisher the book by a certain month. Once you promise that, you kind of trick yourself into working. And also I think I'm really lucky, in a sense. I can write what I want to write, and publish books, so I really cherish this type of opportunity. I have a lot of friends in China, some without even time and energy to write; they have to make a living. It's very difficult to be a writer nowadays, everywhere in the world. There are some who cannot write for political reasons, cannot write what they want to write, so in that sense I'm really lucky.

When we first met in 1988, you were studying poetry. I couldn't have imagined that you would end up as a novelist. What did you foresee for yourself back then?

I did not see myself as a novelist or a mystery writer, no. Poetry was the career I had in mind, yes.

So how did it happen that you ended up writing mystery novels?

I remember you and I discussed poetry with each other quite a lot. I remember you said, "Your poetry shows a lot of narrative tendency." We did not really elaborate on that. But that was something. Another thing I'm more positive about is that at one point you were editing a newspaper or magazine, *Tornado Alley*, right? And I wrote a long poem. You remember the title?

"Don Quixote in China."

Exactly. I think that poem partially came to me after my first visit to China after I had been in St. Louis quite a few years. I was impressed by all the changes there. I wanted to write about the society at large. It's not a personal poem. It got a good response from readers. But I was not really satisfied, because I wanted to say more about what happened in China, in what direction the country might go, and reflect on the changes. And I felt a little bit restrained when I tried to express all these things in poems. That long poem, it's a narrative, it's a little like a story, and I thought, maybe I can write a story for a change. And that's how I think the first idea about a novel came to me. And then I don't know how I really worked it out—one thing just led to another.

At that time you were running a translation service.

Yes. And I was not that busy. You cannot translate all the time. So sometimes you sit and you don't want to waste your time, right? So I spent more and more time on the manuscript. But I did not even know at first that it was a mystery. It's just a book about China, my response to what's happening. With poetry writing I took so many classes. But with the novel I did not. So I had a hard time putting the chunks together, organizing the thing. I liked mysteries, so I thought I could use that format. And I tried that. I did not know whether that would work or not, but my SoHo [Press] editor told me it worked.

And there you are, a mystery writer.

They wanted me to sign a contract for three books. You can understand I was happy. After that I had no choice; I had to write a second and third one! Hopefully I have a little more choice nowadays.

Do you still write poetry?

I still write poetry. I still have Inspector Chen write poetry. Sometimes I even have other characters in the books write poetry. In *Red Mandarin Dress*, even the murderer writes a poem. I like the poem, but it's kind of creepy.

You could live anywhere you wanted to. So why do you live in St. Louis?

I like St. Louis. I don't know whether I could be quite as productive living in New York. So many things happen in New York. In St. Louis, the good part is that while you are in St. Louis, there not too many distractions, right? (*Smiles.*) Nowadays I travel quite a lot, so I probably won't feel bored. I'll be going away May first. I'll be back probably in June. Then I will be gone again for the whole month of October. That will be at the Singapore Writers Festival. And then there will be an Italian seminar on the mystery novel, and that will be in Beijing, and before that I may go to Germany for another festival, and I may have to go to the Frankfurt Book Fair that's in October. And I always stop in Shanghai, to relax, to eat out. My sister is still there, and also one elder brother. He is paralyzed. He's in the hospital. It's like a nursing home but not exactly; it's a hospital. So I need to visit there and to pay the bills. Back home in St. Louis, you just—you just work. So I think it works out for me.

St. Louis is a good writing environment.

A good writing environment, yes. My daughter I talked to just a few days ago. She's in New York, shopping, and I said to her, "Are you are coming back to St. Louis?" and she said, no way. (*Laughter.*)

When you go back to China, how are you treated? You were once worried about going back because of what might happen. But now that you're successful in the Western world, are you treated differently? Does the government keep an eye on you while you're there?

They keep an eye on me, I'm sure of that. But so far I have not got into any trouble. I also have been very cautious. My friends, my acquaintances, my relatives, they of course treat me, I hope they can treat me, still as someone "inside," residing in China all the time. But they cannot help it, they treat me like someone back from the States. That part I don't like so much. But I don't think, because there are so many things going on in China right now, that the government would really single me out. I've gotten a word of advice, a warning from time to time, "Be careful," something like that, but nothing formal or official.

Last time you went to China it was specifically to do research. What were you researching and where?

I went to a city not far from Shanghai, Wu Xi. Wu Xi used to be known for its lake, called Ti Lake. But in recent years, because of pollution, people cannot drink from it, and the lake is covered by green algae. I think the whole city ran out of water, and for a couple of weeks it was national news. I wanted to see with my own eyes how bad things were. And I stayed there and did some research there.

People must say all kinds of things to you: congratulate you, ask where you get your ideas, give you praise, want to shake your hand, say they've read your books. What do you wish people would say to you?

As a writer, if people tell me they enjoy reading my books, or they tell me they had fun reading a book, or they learned something, that's all I want. It's not something like praise. That, to me, is irrelevant. But it's what you have done: you have given joy, or given some information to the reader. So that means your labor was not wasted.

And what do you wish you could tell everybody?

Well, Inspector Chen in the books becomes more and more realistic. Maybe a little bit cynical. He can only do what he can do. I can't live like him. I write books, mainly at this stage books about China. But maybe writing about China in a way no other Chinese can do. I'm in quite an advantageous position compared to some American writers, including some Chinese writers here. They also write about China, but very few, almost none, go back to China so frequently and can have access to what's happening right now. In a way I hope that mine is a kind of a double or combined perspective. I'm still inside, but I'm also outside. And also I think in this global age, it's not just about China, but it's general, universal. Like the book I'm working on about pollution. I'm trying to go to the root of the problems. Of course at the root one can always say one thing and be right. But that's not only in China; it's the same thing here. Five or 10 years ago, a lot of Chinese intellectuals took the capitalist system here as a model and believed that once you adopted this system, every problem can be solved. But it's not the case. So a lot of things you can call universal. It's not just China or the United States.

You say that you're in but you're out. Did you decide to take American citizenship?

I'm already a citizen. Long time.

I remember the struggle to get you a green card.

Yes, it was a struggle. Especially the way I had to swear. Some people took it not that seriously: "Okay, it's just words." To me, it was serious. One thing I thought about before I decided to take American citizenship was that I knew I would have go back to China because of my books, and I didn't know, if I still held on to my Chinese citizenship, what would happen when I went there. I thought about it.

I'd like to hear whatever it is you'd like to tell everyone.

I think I've been very lucky.

If you could identify one important turning point in your life, what was it?

Nineteen eighty-nine. Before that I wrote in Chinese and never thought I would pursue a career as an English writer. That's definitely a turning point.

Jane O. Wayne

POET

THE STARTLES TELL US

No effort at all.
You simply stumbled
    upon that room, but the next night
when you searched,
the door was gone
        so you couldn't get back
to details—the color of a wall
   or carpet, the pattern
of upholstery.

   You moved on instead—
the passenger who steps off
a subway train
       in an unfamiliar station
and doesn't know
which way to turn—another day,
another platform—everything
   in flux, dizzying,
even the self
       fluid as a face
in a damp mirror,

    your own legs wavering
below you in a pool,
the mind, too, always revising itself.
          Suppose next
you lose your handwriting or the color
in your hair,
    then what about
your tastes—do you take it with
        or without sugar;
and which shirt, which way home?

On the hill, none of this
    matters when the wind
returns a branch
to the ground,
and that sudden thud
        returns you to yourself
   in time to notice
the dry whisper
of the Eucalyptus leaves, a crescendo
    spreading through an orchestra.

J ane O. Wayne has to be sought. She is not a public person. Author of three books of poems, Wayne is usually either at home, a cozy and soundless place where she writes in her second-floor study, or she is traveling in far-flung countries: Albania, Vietnam, Guatemala. These poles of experience fuse in her work. Short and simply worded, her poems hallow mostly domestic things and scenes that most of her readers might think too ordinary to notice: a coat in a closet, neighbors' voices, a window shade:

At the zenith
of rolling up the window shade
there's a falling into place,
a soft snap
when the winding mechanism
catches hold,
pawl in ratchet,
and the taut pull-string
loosens in your hand
so you can let go. . .

From "When It Lifts" in *From the Night Album,* San Antonio, TX:
Pecan Grove Press, 2007.

In her universe, "moments of honey" drip from a spoon, and an everyday suburban living room is exposed for what it truly is, "a room borrowed from time." Wayne says that as a poet she "reads the world," articulating and solving the mysteries in what others take for granted. A new poem appears for the first time here, chosen by Wayne from the manuscript of a forthcoming book, titled *The Other Place You Live.*

Jane Oxenhandler Wayne married painter Sam Wayne in 1963. They had two children. Except for a short time in Manhattan and trips abroad with her husband and family, she has lived in suburban St. Louis all of her life, earning her B.A. and M.F.A. at Washington University. Her first book, *Looking Both Ways,* won the Devins Award and was published by the University of Missouri Press in 1984. A portion of her second book, *A Strange Heart* (Helicon Nine Editions, 1995) is about Sam Wayne's heart transplant and eventual death, but from the poems this would be hard to guess. Her poems are voiced not by a personality but by a presence. It has a level gaze and a level temperament. It never looks away or falters. Seemingly effortless, each poem is achieved by extraordinarily hard work, daily and at all hours. Wayne, who studies Latin, keeps in mind the motto *ars et celare artem:* "Art is to conceal art."

Wayne's work has been published in journals such as *Poetry, The Iowa Review, The American Scholar,* and *Ploughshares. A Strange Heart* won the 1996 Marianne Moore Prize and the 1997 Society of Midland Authors Poetry Award. *From the Night Album* (Pecan Grove Press) was published in 2007. As successful a poet as Wayne is, she is not worldly. In person she is a composition artfully dressed in textured fabrics and worked silver. Her study's window opens into the dark spokes and drapery of a tall evergreen. Conversation unearths unlikely nuggets of unease. She will autograph her books, but explained to me that she quit inscribing them because she once unwittingly bought by mail a used copy she had inscribed to a personal friend.

"I have this very strange feeling that I'm never writing," Wayne said. "When I'm starting a poem I don't know if I have anything because all I might have is a fragment. And I keep working on it, and I think, 'I'm just working on something that I thought of earlier.' And when I finish a poem I think, 'Well, I wrote that earlier.' So I really never think I'm productively writing. Nothing anybody says can reassure me. I'm deeply insecure. I'm not good at talking."

Not everyone wants a public life. Not everyone is cut out for it. But in this interview, done in her study, Jane Wayne opens the door for a while, and steps out.

"That's the Real Reward"

CATHERINE RANKOVIC: *Is this your writing room?*

JANE O. WAYNE: Yes. This is a multipurpose room, but it is where I write. I'm really a creature of habit. We've lived other places, but I always find I cannot write in other places. The year we lived in Reading, England, I wrote one poem, and I was working every day. I just couldn't produce.

So you have to be home?

I'm a real homebody. Basically I'm very shy. I assume everyone else is. I don't know if they are, but I always go under that assumption.

I think what makes writers is a communications issue that develops very early, and the writer spends the rest of his or her life trying to communicate.

I just know I've always felt like an outsider. I think each book I've written has characters in it, people who are not me, but people I certainly identify with and I imagine into them: loners. Like a bag person. That seems so far-fetched, that a middle-class person would identify so heavily with fringe figures. But we are who we are, and it may not seem congruent.

When A Strange Heart *won the Marianne Moore Prize in the '90s, and* From the Night Album *came out in 2007, almost nobody heard about them. You didn't issue announcements or press releases.*

I'm really not good at the world thing. And I hate teaching. People don't understand that. It seems so reasonable to me that people would not want to be up there performing every day. For the longest time I didn't think I could bear public readings. I remember Connie Finkel—Constance Urdang—was one of my friends, and like a mentor; she was older than I, although I never studied with her. But she had the same feeling about giving readings. She got over it. She was always telling me those things were necessary. But her husband Don was really my primary mentor.

I know you went through the Washington University graduate M.F.A. program, graduating in 1977.

It's probably true. How time flies! It seems so long ago.

And Don Finkel was one of your teachers.

Yes, and Howard Nemerov. I had had John Morris for literature courses, not writing. He was on my master's thesis committee. On occasion he read my work and went over it with me.

I would think that you and John Morris would have a lot in common artistically.

I really like his work. It's inimitable, though. I don't know how he did what he did. But I'm a great fan. John was so self-effacing. I liked that very laid-back quality he had. I think all the people I admire weren't flashy. It was before that kind of rock-star image came about.

About when do you think that was?

Oh, I don't know. There's been a sea change. It's nice to witness it. If you live long enough, you understand what our elders once thought, as they looked with incomprehension at what we were doing. It's kind of nice to reach that misunderstanding.

Where's your hometown?

St. Louis.

And what neighborhood did you grow up in?

Oh, shameful. Ladue.

Shameful?

It's a lot to overcome. That's what made me an outsider. Oh, it was very exclusive then, and I always felt that I didn't fit in. It was very—it seemed very repressed: emotionally and psychologically repressed. You know, the '50s. It was horrible. Then came the '60s.

I had read about you going around the world in a freighter and visiting—

Wonderful places.

Was that in the '60s?

We were married in '63, and I think we went in '65-'66. It was wonderful.

Really? Life on a freighter is wonderful?

We crossed on the freighter, and after that we would stay at very crummy places, and hitchhike, and take third-class rail in India, which is—well, I don't know if I'd wish that on everyone, but it was such a learning experience. It just turned me right around. There were no assumptions that I could make after that—cultural assumptions.

Were you hippies?

I think of a hippie as being more reckless. I've always been security-minded. It was a very difficult thing for my husband to give up his job. We were both teaching, the last time I ever taught full-time, in a high school. It was more like being a jailer in those days.

What was your husband's name?

Sam Wayne. He was a painter. That's a picture of him. He was a marvelous person. He built the furniture downstairs; he could do many things.

Looks like that photo was taken overseas.

It was taken in Nepal, when it was Nepal. It feels like everything is so different; it's so accessible now.

What other jobs have you held? You say you taught high school?

For however long it was before we went away. And that's it. I mean, I worked in New York doing secretarial kinds of things, but I've really been a full-time writer—and apologetic.

Apologetic?

You know, everyone says, "What do you do?" meaning, "How are you gainfully employed?" and I have been a writer. That's been hard. Maybe it's just something I've struggled with within myself. I've had good fortune, and I've had to live in a very careful way to make ends meet on one salary. I viewed that as my work: going to thrift stores, cooking beans, and saving every penny.

Psychic income, they call it.

When you have young children, it's hard work. I would take them to school and immediately come home and start writing. Or if somebody else drove our carpool and I was still in pajamas, I would go to the computer until they came home. I would eat standing up with a piece of bread and a piece of cheese, and rush back upstairs. So I really treasured that time. It seemed like a lifeline.

It was a long time until you got a book published.

Ten years. That's the way I look at it, a book each decade. My late husband would say, "Vermeer only did 64 paintings in a lifetime, but what paintings!" So I thought, we're working for quality, not quantity. But now I have written a manuscript in a very short time and am trying to get it out there.

You have a new one?

Yes. I think I'm sort of writing—well, the way I've always written. What's being published is a lot different now.

How so?

It's unfathomable. I just think, "Huh?" I still have old-fashioned ideas about writing clearly—even when invoking mystery and asking the big questions. My focus is to try to write clearly, which I guess is outmoded now.

What's your family background? Any writers in the family?

I have a cousin who was an academic, retired now, and he published a novel and did critical work on Baudelaire and Cocteau. Another cousin has published a book of poems. And another has written poetry and has written essays for *The New Yorker*. Then there are a few artists.

How about your parents?

(*Laughs.*) Oh, no. That's where I became an outsider, I think. They didn't understand. They wouldn't understand. So I certainly was not writing to please them.

What did they want you to do?

Oh, marry. Have a bourgeois life. So. It's all worked out all right.

When and how did you first begin to write?

When I was very little. I was writing little journals, diaries with locks and keys, having a notion that one should write about something secret that you wouldn't tell anyone else. Then I began to read poetry. When I was a child someone gave me the book *Gift From the Sea* by Anne Morrow Lindbergh. Now I look at it and I think, ha, but that way of living, slow living, and contemplation, is something I learned from that book very early on and strove for.

Have you tried other arts besides writing?

No. But I think living is an art form. When I get dressed every day I'm very aware of the colors I wear, of everything in my house and the placement of it, putting flowers on the table; I'm very concerned with esthetics. I got that from my mother. She was very sensitive to the beauty of things. I love to sit here and look at that fir tree, limbs dangling. It's absolutely gorgeous, and what's so amazing, it hasn't always been there. It was a little Christmas tree that we planted, and each year the branches are at a different height outside my study window.

So it keeps you company.

It's something to contemplate.

It's so very quiet here in your room. And you're alone all day. That's the way you like it?

I love it that way. Bear in mind that my husband's studio is overhead, and that presence is very important to me, that silent presence. Both of my husbands have been painters and relatively quiet. I'm very much a married person. I'm very much that sort of animal.

You're a homebody but at the same time you engage in world travel.

I've craved it my whole life. I have a great need for change, which is at odds with staying home focused on a monitor or page all day. At other times I'm just a bouncing ball. I've always felt that need to break the pattern, to have a surprise. Often when I'm writing I'm hoping something will surprise me. When words surprise me, or I have a thought that surprises me, I am so excited! The other day a poet friend and I got together and we had just finished poems, and it was so congruent; we were both elated at having finished something. There's a kind of high in having accessed that part of your imagination, and pleasing yourself. That's the real reward in writing. That's the biggest thrill. It sounds very solipsistic, but one wouldn't do it otherwise. There has to be something intrinsic in the process that is so rewarding it carries you through all the difficulty of revising.

And with the other kinds of expense that come with being a poet, such as difficulty publishing, difficulty making a living—you deserve to please yourself. If anybody has a right, poets do.

When I had my first book accepted for publication—I was at a friend's pool in the summer, and my husband phoned me to come back home because I got a call from the press, and I knew what that meant—I thought: "Oh, now I can die in peace." I felt relieved that now when people asked me what I did, I had an answer: "I write." There's something very special about that first writing. It's unadulterated. It's purely for yourself. And for me it was a long period of learning. I think I had a very slow learning curve before I got the courage. But I've taken more risks, I'm being more courageous. And that has been inspiriting—and rewarding. It's been like opening a door.

A door?

I'm obsessed with not being able to find doors. It's like a dream image: Looking for something that maybe really doesn't exist. As if somewhere there's a door that would open onto knowledge. It's the same thing with travel. You turn over one stone, there's another. I think the worst thing would be to be jaded. But I think that's an aspect of depression, which is something I've struggled with. When you feel flat. So then your writing looks flat. My big test is that I'll look at someone else's work and if that looks flat, then I think, okay, it's me. Nothing is singing anymore. Still it's a problem not to be so hard about your own work that it's disabling.

How do you get through that?

Well, I don't stop writing. I can remember days when all I had was maybe a phrase, and that felt pretty good. I sort of announced not long ago that I wasn't going to write anymore. After we got back from our trip to Guatemala in January [2009], the dead of winter, the trip hadn't taken off the onus of the gray and the cold, which I hate; it's taken me seventy years to realize I must have that seasonal affect sensitivity—I thought, I'm not going to write until it comes to me. Then I thought, how's it going to come to you if you're not there? You've got to meet it halfway. Don Finkel said, "Turn to another art form. Do something with your hands." Well, I've always cooked. I would try to do recipes, hoping there would be some alchemy in a recipe. Or decorating. You know, three objects in a room, where are you going to put them?

You have a fascination with objects. It's almost as if you were a painter yourself. You see things and make them speak.

That's absolutely what I'm after. I look at the world as a book that has to be read. If something strikes me about those branches in the wind, what is it? Why does that, on an unconscious level, make my heart beat a little faster? Why is the sunlight falling on it so magical? There's this exploration that goes on, reading the world. I also think that if I get something right, other people will get it. They will say, "I've noticed that too."

In some sense your poetry seems to be haunted.

With what?

It's a haunted world. There are few human figures in it, and they don't speak. There are objects and observations in your poems, but by no means do we get to know you at all.

That's interesting. I have succeeded in effacing myself. I have a horror of—somebody said my last book was confessional, and I thought, "What?" I may talk about grief. *A Strange Heart* is about my husband's heart transplant. But I don't think of that as confessional. I think confessing is telling a secret.

What I was saying about "haunted"—everything echoes.

Oh, good.

Acknowledgments

I thank first the interviewees, who gave their time and then their permissions for PenUltimate Press to print samples or excerpts from their works and to use their photographs. Many thanks also to the literary executors of Donald Finkel and John N. Morris: Tom Finkel and John J. Morris. Special thanks to Sarah Smith-Frigerio at Washington University, who located Mr. Morris.

I thank the editors of the periodicals in which these interviews first appeared.

The late Robert H. Kneib, another St. Louis writer, was the first to volunteer to read and comment on this manuscript. Winnie Sullivan, the publisher, encouraged me to add the interviews I told her I'd wished I'd done. Four of my students at Washington University—Katherine Comfort-Mason, Kristine Helbling, Kim Burfiend, and Karen Schwelle—helped me extract from the universe the right title for this book. A thousand thanks to my Washington University officemate Marsha Hussung, and my close friends the Doves, the Gunns, the Leaches, and the Rhodenbaughs for their concern and friendship. Thank you, Lillian Vicentijevic, for supporting your local writer.

Washington University, my alma mater and employer, as "The Harvard of the Midwest" attracted and educated many in St. Louis's large and friendly literary community. "Wash. U." and other area institutions deserve thanks for supporting the arts. Thank you, too, St. Louis and the beautiful state of Missouri. I am glad I live here.

All honor to Left Bank Books, the city's sole independent bookstore during most of the era covered by this book, and a friend to all writers.

CATHERINE RANKOVIC

Credits

The interview with John N. Morris first appeared in *River Styx*.

The interviews with Eric Pankey, Harper Barnes, Tess Gallagher, and Jean-Claude Baker, and the profile of Donald Finkel, are reprinted with permission from *The Riverfront Times*.

"Interview with Gerald Early," reprinted with permission from the Spring 1997 issue of *Gateway Heritage* magazine, vol. 17, No. 4, copyright © 1997 by the Missouri Historical Society.

"Interview with Ntozake Shange," reprinted with permission from the Winter 1995-96 issue of *Gateway Heritage* magazine, vol. 16, No. 3, copyright © 1996 by the Missouri Historical Society.

Interviews with Eddy L. Harris, Kathleen Finneran, Qiu Xiaolong, and Jane O. Wayne are copyright © Catherine Rankovic.

ACKNOWLEDGMENTS FOR EXCERPTS AND AUTHOR PHOTOGRAPHS:

Jean-Claude Baker, excerpt from *Josephine: The Hungry Heart*, by Jean-Claude Baker and Chris Chase. Reprinted with permission of Jean-Claude Baker. Photo credit: "Josephine Baker and Jean-Claude Baker in Berlin, 1971," photograph courtesy of the Jean-Claude Baker Foundation.

Harper Barnes, excerpt from *Blue Monday*. Reprinted with author permission. Photo credit: Durb Curlee.

Gerald Early, excerpt from *Daughters: On Family and Fatherhood*. Reprinted with author permission. Photo used with permission of Gerald Early and Washington University Office of Public Affairs.

Donald Finkel, "Hands," from *Selected Shorter Poems*. Copyright © Tom Finkel. Reprinted with permission. Photo used with permission of Tom Finkel.

Kathleen Finneran, excerpt from *The Tender Land: A Family Love Story*. Reprinted with author permission. Photo used with author permission.

Tess Gallagher, "Women's Tug of War at Lough Arrow" from *Amplitudes: New and Selected Poems*. Copyright © 1987 by Tess Gallagher. Reprinted with the permission of Graywolf Press, Saint Paul, Minnesota. Photo credit: Brian Farrell.

Eddy L. Harris, excerpt from *Still Life in Harlem*. Reprinted with author permission. Photo credit: Catherine Rankovic.

Eric Pankey, "In Memory," from *Apocrypha*. Reprinted with author permission. Photo credit: The Center for Book Arts, New York City, 2007.

John N. Morris, "To Julia, in the Deep Water," from *A Schedule of Benefits*. Copyright © John J. Morris. Photo credit: Catherine Rankovic.

Carl Phillips, "Compass" from *Cortege*. Copyright © 2002 by Carl Phillips. Reprinted with the permission of Graywolf Press, Saint Paul, Minnesota. Photo credit: Catherine Rankovic.

Ntozake Shange, "Where the Heart Is," from *Ridin' the Moon in Texas: Word Paintings*, by Ntozake Shange, copyright © 1988 by the author and reprinted by permission of St. Martin's Press, LLC. Photo credit: Frank Stewart/Black Light Productions.

Jane O. Wayne, "The Startles Tell Us," copyright © Jane O. Wayne, published with author permission. Photo credit: Gerard Hanewinkel.

Qiu Xiaolong, Part 4 of "Don Quixote in China," copyright © Qiu Xiaolong, published with author permission. Photo credit: Catherine Rankovic.

About the Author

Catherine Rankovic's poetry and essays have been published in *The Iowa Review, St. Louis Magazine, The Missouri Review, River Styx, 13th Moon, Margie, Boulevard, Natural Bridge, Delmar, Gulf Coast* and other journals. Formerly a newspaper journalist and magazine editor and columnist, she earned an M.A. in literature from Syracuse University and an M.F.A. in poetry writing from Washington University, where she has taught creative writing since 1989 and was a Graduate Teaching Fellow. She has also taught graduate writing courses at the University of Missouri-St. Louis. She has won prizes from the Midwest Writing Center, the Missouri Arts Council, and the Academy of American Poets. Her books include *Island Universe: Essays and Entertainments* (2007) and *Fierce Consent and Other Poems* (2005). Essays appear in several anthologies including *Are We Feeling Better Yet? Women Speak About Health Care in America* (2008), *Guilty Pleasures: Indulgences, Addictions and Obsessions* (2003), and *Memories and Memoirs* (2000). She is an active member of the St. Louis Writers Guild, the St. Louis Poetry Center, the St. Louis Publishers Association, and the women's poetry workshop "Loosely Identified." She writes a blog called "The Confident Writer" (catherinerankovic.com) and advises writers on manuscript editing and publishing. Email: clrankov@gmail.com.